THE HENRY L. STIMSON LECTURES SERIES

Breaking Democracy's Spell

JOHN DUNN

Yale UNIVERSITY PRESS/NEW HAVEN & LONDON

Yale University Press books may be purchased in quantity for educational, business, or promotional use. For information, please e-mail sales.press@yale.edu (U.S. office) or sales@yaleup.co.uk (U.K. office).

Designed by Mary Valencia.
Set in Adobe Caslon type by IDS Infotech, Ltd.
Printed in the United States of America.

Library of Congress Cataloging-in-Publication Data
Dunn, John, 1940–
Breaking democracy's spell / John Dunn.
pages cm.
Includes bibliographical references and index.
ISBN 978-0-300-17991-0 (alk. paper)
1. Democracy—Philosophy. 2. Legislative power. I. Title.
JC423.D8 2014
321.8—dc23 2013037724

A catalogue record for this book is available from the British Library.

This paper meets the requirements of ANSI/NISO Z39.48–1992 (Permanence of Paper).

10 9 8 7 6 5 4 3 2 1

For Anastasia

CONTENTS

PREFACE

This is a very small book on a very large subject. I had the effrontery to tackle the subject directly at all because Yale did me the honor to invite me to give the Stimson Lectures, and I thought it right in response to express as sharply and clearly as I could the conclusions I have drawn from two decades of thinking about the passage of democracy in all its senses around the world. This has not been a comfortable experience. Some of that passage has been inspiring and some of it chilling. Some of its consequences have been very good. Some very clearly have not. It would be nice to believe that the good consequences were natural and readily predictable, and the bad ones surprising and due to purposeful abuse of the term or concept or clear misunderstandings of what it implies. It would also by now be very foolish to believe anything of the kind. What I have tried to show in this book is how to distinguish the political force of the category in our struggles to shape and reshape our lives together from its very limited capacity to clarify our political choices. There is nothing illusory or inappropriate about that force, but it is a limited and critical force against fairly feeble rivals as grounds for authority. It is not a cognitive force in face of the need to judge, choose, or defend our judgments or choices. We have not been judging or choosing very well together for some time. We are unlikely to do much better until we improve our understanding of just why that has been so.

Small though the book is, I have incurred many debts in the work that underlies it. I would like to acknowledge the generous help of colleagues and friends, especially in recent years in Cambridge, in King's College (Stephen Alford in particular), and in the Department of Politics and International Studies (Andrew Gamble and Duncan Kelly most of all). It is very much a book for Yale, which has been a warm and invigorating academic home for me on many occasions over the decades and where I have many valued friends, some from long ago, like Jim Scott, Ian Shapiro, and David Bromwich; some I first knew elsewhere, like Cynthia Farrar; and some I first met relatively recently, like Karuna Mantena, Bryan Garsten, Frances Rosenbluth, and Tatiana Neumann.

The largest intellectual debts behind this book go far back in time and are, above all, to those who taught me (especially Moses Finley) or with whom I have thought and taught intensively for long periods, especially the incomparable Istvan Hont (now tragically gone forever), Raymond Geuss, and, farther back, Quentin Skinner. I also owe very much to those who especially share my interest in the fortunes of democracy, notably Sudipta Kaviraj, Sunil Khilnani, Adam Przeworski, Richard Bourke, Takashi Kato, Takamaro Hanzawa, and the late Kan'ichi Fukuda and Guillermo O'Donnell. The biggest costs of the book were borne, as ever, by my daughters; they will have to judge those for themselves and forgive them if they can. To Ian Shapiro, I owe endless warm hospitality, the opportunity to give the lectures themselves, more than one very happy spell at Yale, and many wonderful conversations on evening after evening.

My weightiest debt in completing it is to Anastasia Piliavsky, who gave me the will and capacity to finish it at a very low time and did her best to prune it of innumerable blemishes, most of which I have obstinately retained. To her, her courage, intellectual audacity, power of vision, rage for justice, and incomparable energy, I keenly hope for the good fortune to owe a great deal more.

I am warmly grateful for the support and assistance of Yale University Press, especially of William Frucht and Jaya Chatterjee, for the sensitive copyediting of Kate Davis, and for the two searching and challenging reports that the press commissioned from its readers. One of these suggested that I should write instead a more comprehensive and carefully reasoned treatment of the very large topic I try to address. I decided not to attempt this, because I thought it would blur the focus and diminish the impact of the message I most wish to convey. The second, which caught the spirit of the book with heartwarming generosity, made some careful political criticisms and urged me to try to think further and deeper. I shall be going on thinking in response to it for some time.

BREAKING DEMOCRACY'S SPELL

Introduction

In the societies of the West today we constantly assure one another of our singular good fortune in several distinct but complementary respects. In the teeth of the hideous disparities between our destinies as individuals, families, or classes, we find it heartening to view ourselves as united and blessed collectively by historical good fortune in numerous prominent ways. Some of these feelings, and the judgments that underlie them, are quite well advised. It was luckier for almost any European to have been born after rather than before the

Second World War,[1] and luckier still for a very great majority to have been born after the Second World War than at the wrong point before the First World War.[2] Many of these fond assessments of our good fortune, however, like the sentiments so deeply confounded with them, are very poorly judged. The main purpose of this book is to show how and why they have come to be so, and suggest how we can begin to judge better.

Where does our current sense of historical felicity come from, what does it rest on, and how secure are its foundations? In the first place, we have come to see ourselves as fortunate in the economic arrangements on which and within which we live our lives: Some, to be sure, are distinctly more fortunate than others, but who says life, says luck, and hence perhaps also injustice.[3] In the second place, we feel ourselves fortunate too in the political arrangements under which and within which we live—fortunate in their intrinsic justice and decency—and in the high levels of security with which they furnish us, some of us again more lavishly than others (and there it is harder to view the disparities as natural fatality rather than political choice). In the third place, we tend to view ourselves as more fortunate still in the happy (perhaps uniquely happy) fit between our political and economic arrangements, and in the ease, amity, and mutual respect of the social relations that naturally arise from their happy conjunction.

The economic arrangements in question, we like to imagine, are fundamentally structures of free exchange between individuals, reproduced over time through returns on the investment of capital. (Do not ask where the capital first came from.) The political structures, likewise, are structures of free self-rule by real equals, also founded on free individual choice, exercised on the basis of free exchange of opinion, and kept equal by constitutional guarantee through equal votes in mass suffrage elections. Older guarantees of personal security and civil liberties, embodied with varying density in public law or written out painstakingly in constitutions, undergird structures that are trustworthy in themselves and valuable on other, and at least equally compelling, grounds. The ensemble of these structures, "liberal democracy," as many now call it, does not offer all things to all persons, since human beings continue to vary widely in their tastes and prejudices and no set of arrangements could satisfy all of them all the time, still less ensure that they remain satisfied as history unfurls in front of them. But it is plausibly true that over the last two-thirds of a century, this ensemble of practices has offered more such grounds to more human beings over a larger area than any earlier assemblage of human arrangements. Why then should we not be confident that it will continue to prove able to do so, on an ever-ampler scale and across a steadily widening arena, as far as the eye can see?[4]

This sanguine assessment might be reasonable if two conditions were satisfied and could even be compelling, if we could know two things. In the first place, we would need to know that this happy outcome was fully equipped to ensure its own future continuity in space and time. (For us to know this, it would have to be true that it was and that we had the means to be certain that it was.) In the second place, we would also need to see for ourselves that it was clearly capable of handling the immediate challenges of collective life within and between individual countries effectively even in the present. Since neither condition plausibly holds, however, there are stronger grounds today for us to view it far more sceptically: less as a serene, deeply adhesive, and self-subsistent totality, and more as a complex and largely opaque historical accident, the internal relations of which remain unstable, vulnerable, and replete with continuing danger.[5]

The central judgment behind this book is the extreme urgency for the citizens of the wealthier countries of the West to learn to distinguish better a (predominantly) happy accident from a magic formula projected drastically forward from the recent history of actually existing democracies. Their failure to do so has never evinced a high level of political understanding. In face of ecological degradation, the threat of poorly understood climatic imbalance, the manifold political and economic instabilities of the world trading and financial systems, and the increasingly dysfunctional politics of all the major democratic states and their coordinating institutions, this faith in the vindicatory and directive force of our conception of democracy is utterly misplaced.

What really matters about political ideas is what happens to and through them in political use. There is no single word in the entire history of human speech to and through which more has happened than the word *democracy*, not even the word *God*, though over an even lengthier time the words for God or gods have proved still harder to translate between the languages of the world. At least in the countries of the West, and probably now across the world as a whole, one salient prerequisite for improving political judgment is to recognize just what has recently happened to and through the still sometimes-charismatic but almost never clarificatory term *democracy*.

In this brief book I try to bring into better focus the stark outline of an assemblage of processes, bewilderingly and unimaginably complex in itself, yet also weirdly unified through the quite recent destiny of this single word, the multifarious efforts to translate it intelligibly into an ever-widening array of languages, and the more fitful effort to grasp quite what that headlong diffusion means for the humans who have come within its orbit. From almost any pertinent point of view, that unity is necessarily specious and fantastical, but that is very far from rendering it inconsequential. In one sense, it registers a sort of spell through which the world's political imagination has come to be bewitched. In this guise the most pressing challenge it poses for historians and social scientists, and perhaps even for philosophers, theologians, and ecologists, is to understand how that spell has been cast: to grasp the mechanism that has made it so effective where, when, and how it has proved to be so.

That is an academic challenge, and inevitably more salient and less discretionary for some academic disciplines to confront than it is for others. It also happens at present to be a challenge to which even political science, the most conspicuously implicated discipline, is singularly failing to rise. For most of us, however, it is wholly undiscretionary except where politics in its fearsome entirety is something we can safely and reasonably ignore, whether in revulsion, indifference, or blithe unawareness of the havoc it can wreak on our lives. Sooner or later, in most full adult lives, that blitheness is punctured irretrievably, and it may take decades for anything resembling it to drift back within reach. For anyone today with an ear attuned to that havoc and not paralyzed by what they hear, judging what to hope for, what to fear, and how to act on the basis of those judgements requires us to see what has happened in and through this great torrent of words. Only insofar as we can see this can we hope to judge in any but the most perfunctory and reactive way what, within our own political institutions and practices, it makes sense to trust in and how to distinguish this better from what it would be absurd or all but suicidal to trust in at all. "Put not your trust in princes," has often and unsurprisingly proved sage counsel. How much more trust (and just what kinds of trust) should we place in democracy as a political idea or a specifiable form of government?

In political use, democracy as an idea hovers constantly between credulity and paranoia. Just why has it proved so unstable, and how can we learn to hold it steadily closer to the midpoint between those poles?

One way to begin is to distinguish clearly the different ways in which democracy has figured in this bewildering story. The first is simply as a word; the second as an idea or assemblage of ideas that one word has come to evoke as it moved across the world. The third, by now the privileged reference for most of those who use the word at all, is the range of state forms and subordinate institutions that claim the word as their title and presume the idea it invokes to license their authority. Each way has a history of its own. Each, by now, incessantly invokes both the others, and each is therefore constantly affected by the trajectory of both. None can offer a privileged vantage point from which to survey and comprehend the whole. To see this more clearly, we need to proceed more patiently and very much more carefully.

ONE

Diagnosing Democracy's Power

It is natural today for Americans (and at least tempting for many others across the world) to think of democracy as a synonym for good government. On recent evidence in high places, it is even intuitively plausible to some Americans to assume that this linguistic equivalence somehow carries through to practical causality, so that endowing a very foreign country with the facilities for democracy could somehow automatically generate the capacity for it to govern itself well. To hear that meaning lurking in the word itself may simply be ingenuous, but the practical equation has proved altogether less innocent. One way or another, the modern world's romance with democracy has shed at least as much opacity and confusion as it has light. There is something quite central to the political world we now inhabit that we very conspicuously fail to comprehend, and it is hard by now to miss the fact that one major element in generating and amplifying our confusion comes from the deep unclarity and instability of the master idea through which we seek to take our bearings.

The principal aim of this book is to bring that unclarity and instability into much sharper focus. It pursues that aim first by exploring the sources of democracy's current claim to authority and then by seeking to identify the processes through which that claim has won its in so many ways remarkable ascendancy. On that basis it then attempts to pin down the main mechanisms through which that ascendancy has impaired our collective political judgment. In conclusion, it assesses the resources still open to us to recover our bearings and learn to judge less disastrously in the future.

This is a flagrantly un-American agenda. All that can be said in its mitigation at the outset is that its purposes are far from un-American and in no sense hostile to the people of the United States or the great state that has loomed so large in the destinies of the world throughout my own lifetime, a state that, in my early childhood, in fragile union with the Red Army and the tattered remnants of still-free Europe, saved the possibility of civilized life across the globe at its darkest hour. It required some temerity to discuss these questions so bluntly in a very public setting at Yale, of all universities. No one who studies political science in the United States could fail to register the huge impact, over at least the past six decades, of Yale's great interpreters of the drama of American democracy, most of them still very dynamically alive and still living in New Haven: Robert Dahl, if no longer Charles Lindblom, Robert Lane, and David Mayhew, along with the generations of younger scholars who have followed in their wake, some of whom I proudly call my friends. But it is still appropriate to press these questions under the aegis and in memory of Henry Stimson, a great American statesman in the crucible of postwar reconstruction and a figure who, more than most, was forced by the exigencies of his public responsibilities to view the interests of American citizens in the global context in which their successors will continue to have to live.[1]

A simple formula for the goal of this inquiry is to de-parochialize the understanding of democracy for today and tomorrow—to disentangle the skein of ideas the term now evokes and the political phenomena associated with those ideas, as far as practicable, from the contingencies of local political experience and to relocate them back in the intractably global setting that the term itself so unmistakably occupies.[2] That is not a modest project. Every human being comes from a very small and hopelessly parochial setting and can scarcely hope to succeed dramatically in de-parochializing anything, still less the sources of the allure of the single most powerful political formula in today's world. The sole comparative advantages within anyone's reach in pressing this inquiry are a due sensitivity to the continuing perils of political parochialism in the hectically interactive world we all now live in and a sustained effort to grasp how the ecumenical reach of this charismatic category trades off against the insistent parochialism that each of us necessarily apprehends it to signify and refer to.

In America's case in recent years, that acutely parochial sensibility has done many millions of people very grievous harm, as it was doing by the end of my own first stay in the United States in the mid-1960s, and as it had done in my own country a quarter of a century earlier, by the year I was born. Through the harm it was doing to America's citizens then, it was also at that point, as it is once again now, inflicting massive collateral damage on their enduring human interests. It matters very greatly how the citizens and political elites of the United States apprehend democracy: what it means, what it causes in the world, what was required for it to come into existence in the first place, and what is now needed for it to persist with any security in any given setting. It matters for huge populations of which they know almost nothing, and because it matters so much for those, it has long mattered and will continue to matter for Americans and their children and grandchildren after them.

Why does this word *democracy* now hold such singular political authority? Where is the power that lurks so strangely within it? What exactly is it that modern populations are consenting to when they subject themselves to democracy's sway?

You can hear that question in a number of different ways and try to answer it accordingly. One way to do so is to retrace in outline the story of how it won that ascendancy. But to do that, it is first necessary to address a prior issue: What does the ascendancy itself really consist of? That question has two elements. What exactly is it that has gained ascendancy in democracy's sway; just what is democracy as we have come to understand and experience it? And what is it about democracy that equips it to establish and sustain that sway?

What has gained ascendancy is elusive enough in content but easy to recognize in form. In essence, democracy is above all a formula for imagining subjection to the power and will of others without sacrificing personal dignity or voluntarily jeopardizing individual or family interests. The standing of any such formula is necessarily precarious in political use, since subjection itself detracts painfully from dignity in the first instance, and since it also rationally precludes complete assurance of protecting any interests at all.

You can see the imaginative pressure on the formula at once if you call to mind the fact that three hundred years ago, virtually anywhere the word *democracy* might possibly be written or spoken, it was very close to a synonym not for good but for bad government. It is perhaps a bit strident to claim that democracy four centuries ago was a pariah word. As my friend Quentin

Skinner pointed out to me sternly when I did so refer to it,[3] democracy did, after all, elicit a measure of respect on one prominent occasion from a figure as unlikely as King Charles I of England, though admittedly under some political pressure. No one, however, could readily mistake Charles's sponsorship for unequivocal endorsement. The point he meant to concede was not that democracy on its own was a sufficient condition for, or even a helpful contribution toward, good government, but merely that democracy, painstakingly inserted into a highly constraining structure of countervailing powers, could contribute something distinctive to the mix of benefits that mixed government (government that combined elements of democracy with usually rather more salient and consequential elements of monarchy and aristocracy too) could be trusted to supply, and that under these constraints and these alone, democracy could supply that benign supplement more dependably than unmixed monarchy or unadulterated aristocracy could be relied on to provide it.

That special additive, as Charles identified it in his celebrated *Answer to the XIX Propositions* in June 1642,[4] was liberty, a term of great ideological resonance in England's lengthy history and a value that no English monarchs could safely align themselves against. This was no anodyne concession to politeness by a ruler (in any case not noted for his tact), since there are grounds to see liberty in that rich and diffuse English sense as a fair counterpart to the freedom that the democrats of ancient Athens viewed as the principal benefit of their own democratic way of political life,[5] and since the political setting in which the liberty of democracy featured in England's governmental structure was the elected House of Commons, which Charles had painstakingly prevented from meeting for over a decade precisely in order to free himself from its harassments and obstruction.[6] For Charles himself, whatever else might be in doubt about how best to govern England, what was in no way dubious was who was entitled to do so: who was the sovereign and who must submit themselves to being governed—who were the subjects. It was he who was the sovereign, and all the other native born persons in the kingdom were the subjects; and the gulf between the two was categorical and unbridgeable. As he stood on the scaffold nearly seven years later, in January 1649, he insisted for the last time:

> Truly I desire their liberty and freedom as much as anybody whomsoever; but I must tell you their liberty

> and freedom consists in having of government, those laws by which their life and their goods may be most their own. It is not for having a share in government, Sir, that is nothing pertaining to them. A subject and a sovereign are clear different things.[7]

That is not a tone we are still accustomed to hearing in the English language (still less the American). Yet at any moment when sovereignty is located and applied, Charles was certainly right then; and he must still be just as right today as he was in 1649, even though by that year his own argument had turned so brutally against him. Seen from the receiving end, what sovereignty asserts, requires, and imposes is indeed subjection. Whenever it no longer dares to assert or impose subjection, sovereignty itself has vanished away (not merely been parceled out into a miscellany of vaguely demarcated jurisdictions, as for many purposes it frequently now has). Subjection is an inherently distasteful and degrading condition, most disconcertingly so at the point of incidence—at where it is applied. The special and enduring allure of democracy in competition with other regime titles is not that it better ensures the service of the interests of the citizens. How far it does assure anything of the kind is a complicated and elusive causal calculation across time and space, precariously related to regime form, and one in which democracy has sometimes come out badly wrong and will surely often do so again.

Where the allure really lies is in the reconciliatory offer of the chance to assume subjection for yourself and to share, on notionally equal terms, in selecting the person or persons who is going to deploy it. It is hard (and also sometimes wrong) not to be suspicious of this reconciliatory promise: not to see it quite often in practice as largely a mirage, a vision of water in the desert where the water alas is not there. But the water itself is a real-enough need. What is illusory is where it appears to be—almost within reach. Any theory of sovereignty, any conceivable way of imagining and interpreting what it consists of, why it is there when it is there, and why in some form or other it is genuinely required will overauthorize in practice. It will endorse far more claims than carry any critical validity. It will license more power in wholly untrustworthy hands than a steady vision of what is going on could possibly sanction. Democracy is no exception, and American democracy no more of an exception than any other nation's interpretation or experience. Indeed American democracy's greatest claim to historical distinction, its impressive longevity and spatial amplitude, guarantees that it must have encompassed, as it indubitably by now has, a huge range of excess authorization of the outcomes of sovereign choice. If you want power and attain it on any scale, you cannot also hope to elude responsibility. Every sovereign state, to speak crassly, has blood on its hands. The older and bigger, all but inevitably the more so.

In purely analytic terms, there is no reason to attribute democratic sovereign over-authorization to any distinctive speciousness lurking in the category of democracy itself. It is wrong to defame democracy, though equally wrong to try to shield it from any infamy it richly earns in use. But all of us for the present, at least in countries that distantly resemble the United States in their political arrangements, are caught up in the distinctive imaginative deceptions of democracy and exposed more deeply than we can possibly realize to its particular propensities to over-authorize and distort political and moral orientations as it does so.

There is a need on the part of its subjects to which sovereignty answers: above all, the need to establish and sustain a framework within which they can hope to live securely. But it can respond to that need only by removing from them in practice, sooner or later, any right or responsibility to judge for themselves how the sovereignty itself is to be exercised. Democracy in any defensible understanding (any interpretation that is not explicitly mendacious) restores that right and responsibility, however fleetingly, to every citizen, at least in leaving to them the choice over who exactly is to judge how the sovereignty itself is to be exerted. They personally authorize (however unwillingly or inadvertently) the judge or judges, and their own judgment therefore figures explicitly in the terms of their subjection. Just how legibly it so figures—quite how accurately it calibrates and enforces their judgment—is open to serious dispute in any possible institutional rendering of democracy, and is in fact actively disputed in almost all decisions under democracy in which the citizens (between them) particularly care about the outcome. It is not characteristic of democracy, as Plato and Hobbes each definitively pointed out, that its reconciliatory offer of inclusion is reliably experienced in practice as either soothing or normatively unerring.[8]

Seen from that angle, the reconciliatory benediction of democracy looks to be a very poor bargain, an all but vacuous gesture in exchange for a dismayingly complete alienation of autonomy. In the United States in particular, it violates the intimations of a remarkably wide range of sensibilities, from the Kantian elevation of devotion to equality of respect for every member of an often vividly unedifying species,[9] to the surly defiance of governmental intrusion into any sphere beyond defense of life, limb, and personal property, which extends more widely across the American citizen body and which is especially evinced at present by the Tea Party wing of the Republican Party. To see just why the democratic bargain has come to be so widely accepted in America of all countries, and why its acceptance in that setting has come to seem to so many to be a good reason to believe it uniquely eligible for the rest of mankind, it is necessary to see three elements in close relation to one another: first of all, the drastic need for government that arises out of the practical economic and social organization of the human world as it now is; secondly, the all but complete exhaustion of every rival or earlier reconciliatory formula for motivating the acceptance of subjection; and thirdly, but every bit as consequentially, the degree to which citizen acceptance of subjection is in practice inauthentic—provisional, often insincere or impatient, and always open to decisive withdrawal. That, psychologically, is how citizenship now is, and very plausibly how it always has been and was always bound to remain. If citizenship, then that. This third element in the bargain is perhaps intuitively obvious and always recognized at least tacitly by everyone, though it certainly conflicts sharply with what most of us care to be heard saying. You could say that it is the democratic counterpart to prerogative or reason of state: the unstated intention to breach our own personal version of the social contract whenever we deem fit. In that sense, this tacit contract, with its understandably tacit reservations, is indeed, in a memorable phrase attributed to the late Robert Nozick, "not worth the paper it's not written on."

What grounds the third element, plainly, is the prospectively massive personal inconvenience, sooner or later, of cleaving to the contract in unenvisaged circumstances—a consideration within almost anyone's imaginative reach. But the grounds for the first two elements could not be imaginatively immediate in quite the same way. In the midst of militant anarchy, in downtown Mogadishu or the vast hellhole of the eastern reaches of the Democratic Republic of the Congo, the need for government is apparent enough, but the prospect of its effective supply in any form that it would be sane to trust is utterly implausible. The currency of democracy as a regime name today must be understood in settings where relatively effective government already exists, not where it is conspicuously absent, or on the premise that democracy as a political idea, or any institutional embodiment of that idea, might itself hold the causal capacity to usher effective government into existence anywhere at all.[10]

The idea of vindicating the authority of any particular claimant to governmental power by underlining the pressing urgency of the need for *some* form of effective government—Thomas Hobbes's great idea—wilts in political practice just where it is needed most: where the government is of limited efficacy and faces at least some immediate challenger with vivid appeals to some of those whom it needs to govern more effectively.[11] Once an incumbent government faces serious insurgent challenge, Hobbes's train of thought ceases to discriminate decisively between challenger and challenged and differentiates ever more feebly between them as the challenge rises in intensity.[12] Whatever the value of seeing democracy as a cheaper functional surrogate for civil war, it cannot itself furnish a reason to shift allegiance within such a war or lessen the effort to secure victory for the side to which you feel allegiance.

Just as democracy cannot, except by providential accident, vindicate the territorial scope of any given state, it can only serve to identify the legitimate rulers of a demos, a people, which already views itself as a people, a distinct body of human beings who belong decisively together.

Democracy requires a demos. It requires one conceptually if it is to be a coherent idea. It requires one semantically if it is to be a noncontradictory description of a possible historical segment of the human world. More formidably, it requires one entirely practically if it is to come into existence and persist over time in the world.

How can a demos ever exist? There is a clear but perhaps unwelcome answer. It can do so only where shared sentiments, perceptions, and beliefs arise and persist in time and space, and by doing so, create at least the possibility of a common interest: perhaps even a "General Will."[13] But that is simply the grammar of democracy. What can it tell us about its content?

The interpretations it leaves open are starkly binary. With one interpretation, there cannot ontologically be shared sentiments or perceptions between human beings—only individual sentiments, perceptions, or beliefs. These can be shared only insofar as they lack existential content. They can be shared solely in form. On this view, democracy can only be a *façon de parler*, though it can have a shadowy historical presence when people in a given setting routinely speak of it or write about it as present. It can exist merely as a verbal formula. In that guise, its presence or absence cannot be causally consequential. It must simply reflect, and transmit semantically, causalities that emanate from elsewhere. The drama of politics must be merely a shadow play, not a causal site.

Alternatively, there can be and always are sentiments, perceptions, and beliefs (beliefs with existential content) shared among human groupings, but their scope and valency differ dramatically across space and time. Such groupings can and will share common goods and interests of varying density and centrality to their lives, just insofar as they share sentiments, perceptions, and beliefs. On this view, the drama of politics consists fundamentally in the formation, persistence, and dispersion of groupings that do in this way share, and it is overwhelmingly consequential for human life on any scale beyond the narrowly domestic. The conditions for the formation, persistence, and dispersion of such groupings form the fundamental materials of politics and provide the primary categories of distinctively political understanding.[14]

Supposing a demos is historically present, the government it requires is duly available, and a territorial perimeter and civic membership are each settled at least temporarily, whether by common consent or through political or military exhaustion, it is not difficult to see how democracy on its own can help reconcile a population to the need to continue to be governed effectively. Why, after all, should any population be willing to reconcile itself, not to being governed at all, but to be governed by those who currently happen to govern it? Populations can accept subjection, following Max Weber, on at least three very different bases:[15] They can accept subjection because they see themselves as having good reason to accept it, within a framework of practices presumptively composed of good reasons throughout, an optimistic vision of a process that has been running hard for some little time in the societies in which most of us now live.

They can accept subjection, instead, out of awe—a condition less frequently encountered nowadays, not least in the United States of America, and perhaps never overwhelmingly common or very protractedly sustained anywhere at all. More commonly, they can accept it simply out of habit, because they have done so protractedly already and can barely imagine doing otherwise or have simply forgotten how to. All three bases for accepting subjection (rationality, charisma, tradition) have obvious elements of precariousness. Few civil wars of any violence in a globalized capitalist world are likely to leave tradition in good working order, because civil war is highly disruptive of habit (the longer, the fiercer, and the nastier, the more disruptive). Charisma, however amplified by modern techniques of mass long-distance impression management and media control, is a wasting asset, though it continues to punctuate the political history of most countries at whimsical intervals.

Where democracy has inserted and established its legitimatory sway has been within the historical domain of relatively well-settled government in largely pacified states situated within a dynamically globalizing capitalist economy. One natural way to see just why it has done so in this setting is to view its arrival, in classical mode, as the replacement of two obsolete and inherently implausible, if reasonably concrete and determinate, claimants to rule—a monarchy or presumptive aristocracy or oligarchy of some kind—by a third residual claimant with no special plausibility in itself, always manifestly incapable of ruling as or by itself on any scale and, hence, in need from the outset of a mystificatory proxy to do its rule for it, and one that would thrust the issues of entitlement or capacity to rule beyond any possibility of cognitive accountability. Where monarchs or aristocrats can no longer, as Lenin put it: "go on in the old way," who is left to try to do so but everyone else, the people in their full sovereign indefinition?[16] That is what you see if you view democracy's ascent as the triumph of one form of government over two of its historically protracted predecessors, and the sequence so identified is indeed unmistakably there in the historical record. What is ingenuous is to take that historical sequence as self-explanatory or to interpret its outcome trustingly on its own terms. If we press the question of why the demos, who plainly cannot in practice now rule in the United States or anywhere else, are less implausible claimants to do so than the predecessors they have ousted so decisively, the answer cannot simply be that they are so much harder to get into clear focus or keep in focus if ever you manage to do so.

Forms of government are not freestanding institutional structures that stand or fall with the identity and socioeconomic properties of those who populate them. They are also always elaborated imaginative proposals, certainly embodied in complex organizational arrangements and staged by varyingly active human denizens, but extensively dependent throughout for their stability or vulnerability on the inherent imaginative plausibility of what they propose. The most consequential and elusive political property of the United States, over 170 years since Tocqueville's second volume (1840),[17] remains the force of its own distinctive interpretation of the basis on which the demos, its very own people, exercises its all but unchallengeable rule. By now in the United States that basis has been indistinguishable from tradition for a very long time. It can still blaze into charisma briefly at particular historical moments; and it furnishes the dense web of legal rationality that makes up the nation's public life. Democracy in this very American sense is all things to all persons, and almost all the time. But in most of the rest of the world, by contrast, democracy's sway, where it has been exercised at all, has been far briefer, far less secure, and vastly more heterogeneous in its imaginative rendering. It has had to penetrate much thicker armor and struggle to bring to order far more turbulent spaces. It has faced rivals to its rule which were much more formidable from the outset, and at some points these rivals have come far closer to crushing it definitively. In these settings, it has never felt for long that it was living a charmed life.

And yet it is democracy, not monarchy or aristocracy—its two rival forms of governments from ancient Greece onward—that has somehow won through up to the present as the mandatory basis for interpreting the authority of government across most of the world. Why ever should that have turned out to be so? It certainly cannot have been because of long-gone Greek brilliance, captured in the vocabulary like a fly in the amber. And the reason why it cannot is not merely because it would be impolite or transgressive to say so. In ancient Greece, democracy was not the stable majority outcome of the competition between forms of government for Greek communities, even where they were left to their own devices. It could not have been so, because there was no stable outcome; and no one could readily mistake the relative eligibility of democracy for the clear conclusion of consecutive rational thought conducted in Greek across the classical period.[18] If democracy, in its equivocal contemporary sense, has recently shown itself the fittest survivor in competition between forms of government across the world, a verdict, like all Darwinian verdicts, permanently open to reversal, that necessarily provisional outcome cannot be due to the epistemic felicity or interpretative wealth lurking in this simple Greek triad—monarchy, aristocracy, democracy—or the vocabulary that expresses it.

Where it must lie is in something quite different and decidedly less reassuring—the imaginative potential for identification left fully open by the third term of the triad.

Since that potential is left so fully open, it can scarcely in principle have any elective affinity with either law or reason: law, because it is so pervasively there, at least in any modern society, and because that very presence must at any point stand so clearly against the immediate will of any particular persons, and still more of all persons somehow implausibly compressed together into a notional unity; reason, because it seeks structure, determinacy, and even certitude where the latter proves available, while the demos, because it is presumed to follow its own will by the light of its own mind, repudiates any structure or determinacy that lies beyond the scope of that will or the fitful illumination of that mind, and is ill equipped to muster certitude on any issue of real consequence. Under democracy, the demos ultimately authorizes (or deauthorizes) law, and it monitors and adjudicates the claims of reason to interpret what that law is and what it requires. It does so predominantly through a body of legal specialists, who may have little cognitive respect for, and little imaginative sympathy with, the great majority of their fellow citizens, except where these are playing a part within its rituals long hallowed by custom, as the jury often still does. Over most of the dense web of constraint and guidance through which law falls upon individual members of the society, therefore, the authority of the demos, if present at all, hovers very far back and seldom or never makes itself felt directly.

It is not because we value or expect legality (not because we wish law to rule or confidently expect that it will prove able to) that we have chosen democracy as the one ground on which we can accept subjection, insofar as any of us genuinely do. Democracy is not the rule of law. It does not ensure it, and it is still far from clear that it may not sooner or later to varying degrees preclude it. The rule of law, still more evidently, is not democracy. Its attractions are not those of democracy. Its irritations are not those of democracy. Its dangers are not those of democracy. At most, each of these two is a distinct partial good, with every potentiality to conflict with the other. On balance, the populations of Europe or North America today probably value legality quite a lot more than they do democracy, since its benefits, where available, are both more salient and quite a lot more reliable. Almost anyone, sooner or later, can see and feel the advantages of retaining his or her own property rights, however modest in scope, within the framework of the existing law. Where it offers advantages, the advantages of legality are immediate and comfortingly personal. They accrue to each of those to whom they accrue. By contrast, just what the net advantages of democracy are remains an altogether more speculative judgment. It requires the assessment of very intricate causalities at a considerable distance from the life and experience of any given individual. As Hobbes flamboyantly insisted, almost anyone's personal experience of democracy in action is bound, sooner or later, to come out acutely disconcerting.[19]

What is true, however, and what is of very great moment in understanding democracy's ascent, is that in numerous settings across the world, and most of all in the United States itself, democracy has come to be accepted and understood as the content and basis of an existing regime in which, to a significant degree, law does rule. In those settings, it does not rule through its own inherent power (since it has none). It rules by the more or less grudging consent of those who in fact do. At the very least, most contemporary advocates or partisans of democracy believe it to be largely compatible in practice with the rule of law. Not a few of them also assume, in defiance of logic or conceptual clarity, that it enjoys an elective affinity with the rule of law, just as they assume that it enjoys one with the causal dynamics and normative presuppositions of a capitalist economy. Those assumptions, severally and together, are deeply lodged in the political tradition and ideological sensibility of the United States. But considered soberly, in the abstract and on their own terms, they make singularly little sense.

Over most of the earth's inhabited surface they are very far from capturing the intimations or carrying the authority of such residues of tradition as remain in working order, and they cannot even begin to explain why democracy as an idea (or even a slogan) can possess the momentum to establish the right to govern for anyone at all, still less to generate the capacity to govern effectively anywhere that capacity is not already amply in evidence. In very many different respects, America's espousal of democracy is not a hermeneutic aid to fathoming how the rest of the world sees or feels the meaning of this intensely political concept. For one thing, it confounds systematically and sometimes quite purposefully a very drastic process of power with a competition for allegiance between political ideas. The process of power was one in which a temporarily uniquely rich and potent society settled to the project of remaking the world in its own image, as China's emperors had done on their own impressive historical stage for considerably longer. That process of power was real enough, and it has yet to reach its decisive end, but the competition for allegiance between political ideas was always somewhat illusory, a Hegelian shadow play of flickering images of far more elusive struggles between varyingly frank and confused individuals and political groupings. It was in and through these struggles that democracy as a conception or slogan has scrabbled up the cliff of history. The questions to press are just what has it offered those who have chosen to take it up, and why, when, and where they have done so, they have seen and felt it to carry those offers.

If you see the historical canvas of democracy's ascent in those terms, it becomes clear at once that what it depicts superimposes and intersects very different sorts of processes, each with their own distinctive causalities. You can, if you wish, envisage it as a single process, defined by and in part orchestrated through the spatial passage and temporal vicissitudes of this single word and the prodigious proliferation of human experience that has swarmed around it as it has moved forward and outward from its very distant Greek starting point. That is history as pageantry, with all its terrors and exhilarations intact. To see it that way is not only beyond any individual's paltry competence; it also fails to capture at all what about it really matters. What is at issue here is the answer to two key questions. First, what is the political meaning of that spatial passage and those temporal vicissitudes? In other words, what are their political implications? And second, just *why* have they occurred as and when they have? In other words, what *explains* their occurrence? If you superimpose the two stories, you cannot see either clearly. If you fail to recognize their causal intersection, you condemn yourself to misjudging what does explain them, and you are all too likely to misunderstand their political implications. To recognize this is to register a genuine methodological dilemma, but not necessarily to reach an epistemic impasse. Political understanding, insofar as it proves available at all, insofar as politics really is intelligible even in principle, subsists in and must confine itself to an altogether more modest epistemic register.

The frame in which we need to recognize what has happened in democracy's erratic global ascent is the continuous interrelation of two distinct dimensions, each a decisive abstraction from the full, giddy pageant and trauma of history. Both have prominent idealist elements (as history is bound to if you focus hard and steadily enough upon it). Both pass continuously through the dynamics of the human mind in operation and must be recognized to depend on doing so if they are to be understood at all. Neither has any trace of the ethereal. This setting of democracy's ascent is in the first place the global history of human political experience, a space of which none of us can steadily contemplate or hope to take in the magnitude, complexity, and opacity, but within the cumulative residues of which all of us are now, for better or worse, condemned and privileged to live.

That is the stage of every human life now. There is no longer anywhere beyond or outside it: no dependable historical or geographical refuge, no political or cultural privacy left. A lot of democracy's own instability and opacity, both as a political category and as a political phenomenon, now issues from its being so unmistakably at the heart of this relentless elimination of seclusion. Many anywhere in the world must view democracy's presence or prospective arrival with misgivings; and few anywhere can be wholly confident that it offers them any personal guarantee of safety, prosperity, or existential reassurance. (Think of America's invasion of Iraq from downtown Baghdad.) But no regime in the world today, anywhere there is a recognizable regime, no inhabited space that has escaped the state of nature, is immune to the need to address itself to this term, however open and uninhibited the antipathy with which it views it.

It is easy to see the passage of the word itself as meaninglessly epiphenomenal: an immense flotilla of tiny corks bobbing helplessly around in this great deluge of human experience. But that is not a politically perceptive judgment. Both word and category are far more tightly woven into the fabric of this unfolding story. They catch and carry too much feeling and judgment and shape far too much active political purpose as it moves toward the present. Whatever proves true in the future, even if democracy as a political category or a political value were somehow to be extirpated from every human community in centuries ahead, the political space within which that outcome could arise and the political agents who would bring it about would by now be quite largely creatures of democracy's prior passage as a category. That is why we all now hold such a huge stake in understanding the provenance of the term in its current senses and taking in the dynamics and weight of the experience that has given it this grip upon us.

The second dimension is less hectic in tone and perhaps also analytically more tractable. If the first focuses perforce on the political, social, and economic experience of stupefying numbers of human beings, the second concentrates on a domain where political scientists can feel more at home: on political struggle itself and more particularly on the vicissitudes of political concepts within political struggle. What matters here is not the incidence of political struggle—the forms it assumes, the range of participants it pulls into it, or even its outcomes and their causes. It is what political struggle discloses about political concepts themselves. The dimension we need to capture is the respect in which political struggle constitutes and operates as a set of heuristics for political concepts, testing inexorably their clarity, realism, normative insight, and potential to shape goals and consolidate purposes for possible allies and to subvert the power and deplete the will of adversaries, actual or potential. This too is the space within which democracy has so very recently won its dizzy global eminence, fiercely contested throughout, to be sure, but then in this of all spaces, no concept could ever reasonably aspire to move beyond contest.

It is in this space above all that democracy has most unmistakably shown itself unmatched in the power to recruit allies and quell rivals in face of every other category so far defined in the history of human speech.

If we see those two dimensions—the experience of politics and the structuring of political conflict—as twin facets of a single integrated causal story, it becomes clear at once that the relative analytical tractability of the second is very important. That democracy has won its present eminence in and through the global history of human political experience is just a truism, but the truth that it expresses is overwhelmingly abstract, and the infinite array of concrete causalities that it enfolds could never be clearly known to any human being. Very much of it is irrecoverably lost, and what might still be recovered—even the entire epistemic domain of modern political science, past, present, and near future—is a most unpromising guide to the whole.

If the heuristic that has established democracy's superiority in the present epoch in clarity, realism, and potential to shape goals and consolidate purposes for potential allies and weaken and demoralize prospective adversaries has been political struggle itself, it must be right to see democracy's global comparative advantage in the breadth of the field over which it can solicit identification, and the relative narrowness of the space that it is precondemned to exclude, as illicit, nefarious, or actively malign. This was essentially the appeal of the Abbé Sieyès in the great pamphlet "What Is the Third Estate?" which launched France on revolution.[20] It was also the claim to authority that he advanced on that estate's behalf. Unlike the partisans of monarchical power or the open champions of aristocracy, the political nation as Sieyès conceived it was precommitted to excluding only those who chose to exclude themselves from it, those who claimed and fully meant to stand above the law it invoked and recognized, and to free themselves from the constraints that law imposed by determining its content uninhibitedly for themselves.[21]

In a temporary vacuum of authority, there could not readily be a wider appeal within a given space or for a given population (though the political balance would of course be affected by the numbers of those who claimed the privilege). The breadth of an appeal is no index of its credibility, its sheer power to induce belief. By that measure, democracy is not obviously more charismatic than any other political category. But by that measure it is hard to see how any political category could be charismatic in and of itself, or how even those categories most historically efficacious in inducing belief in one context could hope to sustain it when the context changes, as all political contexts do sooner or later. If the identificatory appeal of democracy is personal and purposefully indiscriminate in the persons whom it chooses to address, that breadth and lack of fastidiousness could be, and often has been, lethally repellent to those best placed to defend themselves. But leveled indefinitely and repeatedly over ever larger spaces, its lengthening sequence of particular defeats has been increasingly outweighed by its raw political appeal. It is hard to see how any rival could press its personal appeal more widely or less discriminatingly or offset a narrower and more discriminating address by anything other than consistently proven efficacy, a necessarily vulnerable title to power in any setting.

The human world has not come to embrace democracy, in the muddled, partial, halting manner in which it now does, because it has come to believe in democracy as a solid and reliable foundation for authority. It has done so because it has come increasingly to disbelieve in any other sort of human basis on which to found it, and to distrust compulsively over time all humanly mediated claims to ground it on some suprahuman basis. We should not see democracy's global ascent as a stunning triumph of credulity or a majestic forward march of justified true belief, but simply as an uneven, reluctant, painful series of surrenders of an immense miscellany of other kinds of belief. This is a familiar-enough picture, plausibly associated with some elements of the European Enlightenment.[22] But it is easy enough to recognize that the picture it offers is not that of the Enlightenment as didactic would-be mentor to mankind, but as nervous prophet of the chilly landscape to come. No one who sees democracy's ascent in that ɔused perspective could sanely suppose that ;, whatever else it does or suffers or is enforced to yield unto in the centuries to come, is a synonym for good government.

Under democracy we may be lucky enough to experience good government, but good government is not a facility that democracy guarantees, either in theory or in practice. Under democracy the responsibility for assessing how far government is in fact good does not rest principally on the government itself, either as a discrete actor or a miscellany of varyingly coherent agencies. Instead, it falls on the citizens at large, and the responsibility for amending its aberrations also in the end falls unrelentingly on those same citizens as a whole. It is rude for foreign visitors to say such things, but it is also incumbent on them to tell the truth as they see it. As it looks at present to a foreign eye—from China, or Iran, or Burma, or Switzerland, or Germany or Norway, or even from England—it is hard to see the citizenry of the United States at present as especially successful in furnishing themselves with good government under their uniquely time-tested and elastic democratic formula. This protracted impasse is not somehow democracy's fault. But democracy, of all political formulas, requires each of us to try to understand why such outcomes arise, and why they sometimes persist with such formidable obstinacy.

Under democracy, unlike most other political rubrics, you cannot blame that outcome merely on the temporary and contingent ascendancy of the nefarious or the congenitally foolish. We the People are the nefarious and the foolish every bit as much as the fine and the wise. When we choose badly, we have no one to blame but ourselves. When we quarrel, as we never cease to, over just who is wise or foolish, virtuous, or ill-intentioned, the common frame of identification and all the authorization it provides drop away, and we are left with very little but our mutual antipathies and contempt.

TWO

Democracy's Ascent

It is hard to exaggerate the singularity and mystery of democracy's rise to a global ascendancy, which, however disputed it may still be, is unmatched by any previous category that purports to shape political experience. In itself, that rise establishes two important points. The first, both analytic and causal, is that the victory it represents has been throughout, in essence and in logic, a fundamentally political process: a political victory won by political means and through the mustering and deployment of political power in all its multifarious modes and configurations. As with any large-scale and protracted political process, much of the shape of the victory issued from heuristics, the seeking out and mobilizing of types and sources of force that were previously latent and unactualized. Historians can trace such processes in retrospect, with the incomparable privilege of hindsight, but no one can show how they must come out. It is hard to explain just why this should be so, but futile to deny the overwhelming lesson of experience that it simply is.

The second point is cautionary and also essentially political. It is the extreme political danger of viewing democracy's current global presence as anything more elevated and predictably durable than a contingent and always largely self-untransparent political outcome. More especially, it is the acute political indiscretion of seeing or sensing within it the reassuring potency (imaginatively derived but nonetheless causally efficacious) of something higher, purer, and safer, descending beneficently on politics from above, to soothe and soften the latter's insistent cruelties and absurdities. That may seem an idle fear, since no one, in America especially, does or perhaps could see any real political process that way. There are certainly few historical traces of any American observer seeing American politics in action in their own vicinity in quite those terms at any point in time. (No one, assuredly, could think of it today as the illusion of the hour.) The disabused realism with which most Americans view their own domestic politics does not reach comfortably across the nation's borders. Beyond those confines, it seldom inclines them to view democracy's global ascendancy as an essentially political outcome of a process, no higher or lower in spiritual valency or existential security than any other political process, from the allocation of places on the U.S. Supreme Court or Saudi Arabian arms contracts, congressional logrolling, or the adjustment of Mafia franchises, to the forging of the Red Cross or Amnesty International or the Society of Jesus or the KGB. (It is not that all political projects are somehow the same or of equal value or worthlessness; but every political process is political in the same way, and the dramatic variations in spiritual allure or material menace between them come at least as much from their ecological settings as from the ways in which they specify or prescind from collective goals.)

It is peculiarly easy for Americans to misconceive or fail to apprehend the political character of democracy's historical advance over the last three-quarters of a century for two very different reasons, neither in any way damaging to the United States as a historical civilization or political actor. In the first place, it is harder for Americans than it is for those at the receiving end to see clearly the coercive character of their own power in use, and hard accordingly for them to distinguish their severely contingent winnings from their just desserts. In the second place, and despite the valiant efforts of their political scientists for a good century by now, it is hard for them also not to sentimentalize the category of democracy itself, and do so with especial ease and lack of inhibition as it passes from spaces where they can see for themselves and about which they know a great deal to spaces much farther away about which they know virtually nothing. Why exactly should that be so? Part of the answer may lie in the extraordinary weight of generosity and hope that so many of America's deepest and most passionate thinkers have poured into this category over the last two centuries. Barring a handful of preternaturally sensitive Puritan ministers, no one in North America poured anything much into the category of democracy before the middle of the eighteenth century, and extremely few had occasion even to mention it.[1] But with the American Revolution, the forging of the new republic, and the long, usually amorphous, and always disturbingly incomplete struggle to rectify the anomaly of that muddled birth and to fashion a decent and honorable form of shared life for all components of the people it had brought into existence, democracy in due course came to be not merely the official regime name for the new republic,[2] but also the vessel on which generations of America's most gifted and engaged writers, thinkers, and social activists lavished their aspirations for a shared milieu of existence for everyone fated and entitled to make their lives within it. In America's domestic politics, that great tide of energy and hope has been pretty effectively blocked for most of those two hundred years and more, and it is not an adventurous judgment that it is effectively blocked now and likely to remain so for the near future. Deep domestic frustration and poorly comprehended external power each exert disturbing pressure on political judgment. In combination, they make it especially hard for an American audience to see democracy's current political presence across the world steadily and accurately.

One way to try to remedy that difficulty is to step outside that imaginative force field and look at democracy's global ascent in a way that detaches it effectively from local political allegiance or appropriation. That strategy demands some defense at the outset, since many may see it as confused or futile. The approach taken here is to track the passage of the term *democracy* across the world and between languages, as it moves out beyond Europe or its North American diaspora, and to read the political interpretations it has evoked in the course of the dramatically disparate vicissitudes in which it has figured with increasing prominence across this ever widening space. In this setting it can, by necessity, only be taken impressionistically and episodically, and no one should mistake the result for the serious intellectual history, which still needs to be done, country by country, language by language, decade by decade, and done by those already sufficiently at ease with the contexts in question to fathom just what has occurred within them.

This huge and barely initiated collaborative task is as urgent politically as it is intellectually. There are very radical antipathies and profound conflicts of interest in today's world (as there have been ever since we can see into human history at any depth), but those indubitable sources of danger to each and every one of us and all that we hold dear are dwarfed in scale and acuity by the towering menace of our massive mutual ignorance and incomprehension. We do not understand the world we so precariously share, and we do not understand it, in very large measure, because of the severely limited degree to which we understand one another or grasp what virtually all the world's other inhabitants really care about or why they care about it as they do.

If that seems a fanciful judgment or a silly preciosity, just turn your mind momentarily to the twin British and American invasions of Afghanistan and Iraq and the terrible harms that are still issuing inexorably from them. But even for someone who took seriously the pressing need to understand these convulsive global encounters, why seek to fathom anything about them by tracing the vicissitudes of a word? There are two reasons to select that strategy of understanding, one distinctly more obvious than the other. The first and obvious is political—the extraordinarily highly cathected political valency of the term in question. But the second and less obvious reason is essentially cognitive. It is the vastly greater epistemic determinacy of what lies at the center of the process being traced.

The history of democracy as a *word* is an exercise in political philology, a severely underdeveloped intellectual practice, even in the wake of the linguistic turn, and one that in the fullness of time and pursued with the assiduity it deserves and requires can, and perhaps in due course will draw on some of the huge intellectual capital of the shaping matrix of the Western mind over almost a millennium, and bring that capital back into active political use. This is in no sense a narrowly occidental intellectual project. It can draw on just as deep a heritage from the civilizations of South Asia or any part of the Islamic world, or of Japan, Korea, or above all China, in Eastern Asia, as it can in the countries of the West. The handful of scholars across the world who are audibly aware of the scale and promise of that task—figures such as the Sanskritist Sheldon Pollock[3] or the Islamist Michael Cook[4]—for the most part still emanate from or reside in the West. But they have always had, and will in the future have on a far greater scale, counterparts, equally gifted and just as keenly engaged, who come from and remain within all the great centers of cultural creation and conservation across the world. What human beings can do in politics depends principally on the institutional structures that confront them or are available to them and on the material environments within which they find themselves situated. But what they try to do and even what they choose to attempt depend every bit as much on how their imaginations work and how they see and feel about themselves and the human world that surrounds them at varying distances. It is because of the unmistakably consequential prominence within that space of democracy as a legitimatory formula that it is now so urgent to take in just what has been happening in and through its passage as a word across the globe over the last two centuries.

The key to democracy's passage through this space is the horizon of identification it has held out to so very many and the basis it has offered them for discrediting and denouncing their immediate enemies. There is no reason to assume that this has invariably enhanced their political judgment or improved their political prospects. Very often, no doubt, it has tantalized them with the promise of a power, control, and efficacy that were largely delusional and led them off defenseless to the slaughter, like some huge global after-echo of the Children's Crusade or replay of the bloodbath of Passchendaele. Consider the tangled outcomes of the Arab Spring or, at a more respectful historical distance, the devastating continental aftermath of the Second World War.[5] But however vulnerable that promise may prove, the power to move very large numbers of human beings is a formidable political factor in itself. And it is hard to overstate the motivating force of the strictly political services that this word has seemed to offer to endless millions of frightened and suffering people, or to exaggerate the consequences of that impact.

To look at political experience through the carriage of power by a word is to view politics from a very odd angle and one that, by itself, could scarcely equip anyone to understand much of consequence about it. Most people today do not think of democracy in the first instance as a word. They view it as a form of government or an assemblage of institutional practices. In the United States, less hesitantly than anywhere else in the world, they think of it as their own form of government and the assemblage of practices that currently defines it. When they ask about the presence or absence of democracy elsewhere in the world, what they principally have in mind is the presence in varyingly distant settings of reasonably good facsimiles of that form of government, and of practices that express values like their own, at least when the latter is on its best behavior. When they go on to inquire how that form of government has come to prevail to the degree that it has in many areas of the world, or even why it initially arose in their own country, and why elements of it had arisen earlier and elsewhere, they look at the formation of states, the techniques of political control, the genesis of resources from human populations and their mobilization by rulers or local power holders, the bases on which groups of human beings can be induced to cooperate or comply with requirements pressed on them from above. These pictures can be cool, detached, and comfortably cosmopolitan. They can read history without disclosing local allegiances within it or assuming that it carries a legitimatory moral that favors some and disfavors others, today or tomorrow. Such approaches make it possible to ask how politics works and doesn't work and why it takes broadly the forms it now does, without precommitting the questioner to reaching answers supportive or even comfortable for anyone at all. There are good reasons for the existence of political science as an intellectual genre and a professional practice. But as soon as you ask which of these forms of government or practices or presumptive purposes and informing principles have merit and deserve allegiance, that hard-won professional composure is instantly ruffled, and the sense of coherent inquiry, and even of consecutive good sense, soon comes into serious jeopardy.

Consider the question of whether it really was the Greeks who invented democracy, where many contemporary Greek citizens emphatically wish to affirm a positive answer, but serious and exhaustively informed students of democracy's history on the other side of the world feel it every bit as essential to insist on a negative one.[6] Those who affirm the positive answer principally wish to claim for their own a historical experience, in some ways glittering enough, in others as ugly as the historical experiences of every other human community, which happens to have occurred more or less where they now live and to have been enacted principally through a language intriguingly continuous with their own. This is an innocent-enough appropriation and not notably more ingenuous than most communities' appropriations from always fairly discrepant pasts. What irks the critics of Greek claims to be democratic originators is not the innocent narcissism of contemporary Greeks, it is the appropriation of effectively the same claim on Greece's behalf by the remainder of Europe and its potent and wealthy diaspora across the oceans. Hence the counterclaim that any specifiable element of what has since come to be called "democracy" had been prefigured or prenamed in other roughly adjacent settings, especially in continental Asia, before the Greeks came to adopt it. It has not thus far proved possible to trace anything very clear or illuminating of what was going on in the favored settings (Mesopotamia, Phoenicia), let alone to pin down its local political significance or demonstrate that it had definite consequences for what the best recorded of Greek communities did to and through the category of democracy. But there is no reason whatever to dispute the passage of cultural and intellectual elements from a wide variety of non-Greek societies and polities to Greek *poleis* in the epoch in which the term *democracy* first came into recorded use, or the possibility of extensive Greek imitation and experimentation on the basis of earlier and clearly non-Greek practices and expedients.[7] It is hard to believe in either case that these are the right questions to ask. Human beings have had to devise ways of taking and lending authority to binding collective decisions on the varying scales on which they have lived together across the world and for far longer than we have reliable descriptions of how they did so. It is scarcely conceivable that there could have been a distinctive and uniquely compelling approach to doing so that occurred to one set of human beings, speaking one language, in one place and at one time, but comprehensively failed to occur to any others elsewhere earlier or later. It is certainly impossible to believe that the practice of assembling to discuss in public what to do did not, on different scales and bases, arise and persist in every humanly inhabited continent and do so well before we have legible records of how the inhabitants dealt with one another on any scale at all. (For words to survive, they need to be legible, and there cannot be legibility without literacy.)[8] It is odd to imagine that we ourselves have somehow chanced upon a vision of how to ensure that when we do come together in person, virtually, or by proxy to discuss in public what to do, we now have at our disposal any more radiantly compelling a conception of how to conduct that discussion in practice on a basis legitimately disconcerting to no one.

What the Greeks did originate was a word, and a word through which, whatever its semantic correlates in other languages beforehand, a lot of dramatic political life occurred within a wide range of Greek *poleis* and most flamboyantly and articulately in Athens itself. It was that flamboyance and articulacy, whimsically frozen in text, that enabled that word to survive the demise of an independent Athens, and even of the cities of the eastern and central Mediterranean, which preserved many of its political forms in outline for many centuries to come. It survived not as an ideological force or a glowing emblem of power, but as an instrument for thinking. Some of that thinking was certainly concerned with ideological force, the sources and modalities of power, or the unsteady relations between power, benign political purposes, and beneficial political consequences. But that concern did not guarantee the benignity or efficacy of power in use or serve in anyone's eyes as assurance of the purity of political purpose. Nor did it suggest any elective affinity between the regime form to which it referred and the quest for knowledge or scientific understanding. If anything, the relation it suggested between this particular regime form and either political merit or cognitive insight was more disjunctive than mutually supportive.

The fact that the single most widely dispersed and potent term in political speech across the world today, and in that sense, because of the relentless growth in the numbers of living humans, the most potent political term there has ever been, survived into today's world at all, not as a focus of political loyalty or normative aspiration but as an instrument of thought, is as startling as it is important. But that fact, of course, does nothing to explain how or why it has come to be so widely dispersed or why it exerts such political potency. To see why it has and does, it is necessary to consider the political history of the world over the timespan in which it has spread so widely and picked up such political momentum.

It is necessary to watch the word carefully as it enters the political repertoire of one country after another, picking up friends and enemies as it goes along, and helping to recompose political coalitions and reshape political enmities as it does. Look at the world in 1750, and it can barely be seen or heard in action even in heated discussion between handfuls of politically motivated intellectuals like Jonathan Israel's emblematic radical heroes, trudging manfully forward in the footsteps of Spinoza.[9] View or listen to it as it leaves the maelstrom of France's Revolution and the ravages of Napoleon's wars of conquest, and already it seems to have hitched its colors to the huge inchoate movement of egalitarian reconstruction that shaped so much of the two centuries that followed but that has now been all but extirpated as an imaginative and energizing political force.[10] While that movement—socialism, or words to that effect—was still expanding territorially, in however erratic a manner, it fully retained the potential to set a drastically different frame and valency on the idea of democracy, and to impose that frame, however clumsily and brutally, on the experience of immense numbers of human beings. But in that form the tide has long ebbed decisively, and all that is left in the word itself is a pallid ghost of the power it once held. What has carried this word so far up the global beach today is to an overwhelming degree one thing—the role it came to play in explaining America's politics to itself.

There is still no very illuminating account of exactly how and why it came to play that role, though Sean Wilentz's *The Rise of American Democracy* comes closer en passant than any other. But there is now reasonably clear agreement among informed scholars that the movement for American independence and the subsequent construction of the new republic were in neither case in any sense political struggles conducted under the banner of democracy or intended by almost anyone to establish that republic as a regime appropriately so conceived in the round.[11] In 1776 *democracy* was simply not a banner word. It was still in close touch with the cool analytical perspective on political existence that had launched it on its lengthy post-Athenian historical career and continued to confine it to narrowly academic or intellectual circles for over two thousand years. Even within that milieu, it was not viewed as a plausible solution to the pressing problems of any community of any scale that recognized itself, willingly or otherwise, to face pressing problems. It was not the solution to the riddle of anyone's history. Within a more analytical perspective, to be sure, it could be employed (and sometimes was employed) to refer to properties of the new regime by those who hoped to usher it into safe and durable existence. In other contexts, some of these apparently positive observers, notably Alexander Hamilton,[12] expressed, before and afterward, a visceral hostility to the political arrangements and turmoil that the word evoked for them and that they expected it to arouse in most of their audience. What held the movement for independence together was a hostility to being subjected to imperial power and authority from the other side of the ocean. In no sense whatever was it a commitment to democracy as a form of government or a political value.

In a few relatively sophisticated cases, its implications soon came to be seen as explicitly republican: hostile by commitment to monarchy as such. For John

Adams, as early as the spring of 1776, "There is no good government but what is republican,"[13] a view he went on in due course to fill out at considerable length.[14] For less decisive and theoretically relentless participants, democracy was certainly no proxy for a republic, and was seen by most to carry very specific dangers of its own. For those with very large stakes in the country, simple democracy was close to pure threat. In Maryland in the same year, Charles Carroll of Carrollton, one of the richest men in North America, saw the prospect of the "simple democracies" he believed his fellow Constitution makers intent on establishing as the worst of all forms of government, and bound to end, "as all other Democracies have," in despotism.[15] For James Madison, from the tenth *Federalist* onward,[16] the prospects for stabilizing and consolidating the new republic rested not on provenly erratic models drawn from a distant Greek past, but on the design of a novel model by a small number of gifted, experienced, and dedicated figures with the political weight and prowess to carry their fellow Americans with them. The great body of supporters or opponents of the new Constitution, he insisted, "must follow the judgment of others, not their own . . . a fortunate coincidence of leading opinions, and a general confidence of the people in those who may recommend it."[17] It was that judgment that lay behind his contributions to *The Federalist*.

By the fourth decade of the next century, when Tocqueville settled down to work out and proffer to the world his own incomparable construal,[18] the new republic had unmistakably embraced democracy in name as well as in substance. Once it had chosen republican independence in place of what it had come to see as imperial subjection, there was little real alternative open to it. There were rich families in the ex-colonies, and among them there plainly were, as there always had been, social pretensions to go along with their wealth; but by 1776 there was nothing there that anyone could durably mistake for an aristocracy, and what dispersed residues of gentility and condescension remained were manifestly incapable of setting their stamp upon the new political order. In the end, despite a few early panics, none even made a serious attempt to. If unmistakably a republic, and a markedly unaristocratic republic at that, what was there for their new regime to be but a democratic republic? And a democracy in due course it duly became, both in its own eyes and, until much later when it met the disapproving gaze of more belligerently holistic egalitarians in Europe or beyond, in the eyes of everyone else who chose to inspect it.

You can disagree (as most now do) with Louis Hartz[19] in seeing this outcome as imparting a distinctive shallowness to American political understanding, which in turn reflected its relatively narrow horizon of social and economic experience. What you cannot readily deny is his insistence that one of its principal consequences was to ensure that the sharpest ideological conflict over the legitimacy of the new order came over its compatibility with a system of unfree labor that required the laborers in question to be excluded from citizenship. That was not an outcome that would have discomfited interpreters of democracy in the communities that first gave referential meaning to the term. But if the war between the states had come out differently, it would have had drastic implications for the global prospects of America's model of democracy in its struggle with professed partisans of equality across most of the rest of the world. Whatever it may have felt like to some of its inhabitants with a fluent repertoire of denial, a slave society cannot readily be seen from the outside as a system of political equality. It is hard to exaggerate the degree to which the global ascendancy of democracy as a category of political aspiration has come from the competitive appeals of equality over those of hierarchy as a category of political identification. Both economic and social equality have further appeals of their own, and it will always remain an open question just how far political equality requires either economic or social equality if it is to be rendered real, and just how far the challenges of economic organization preclude the realization of even the most rudimentary elements of either economic or social equality without prohibitive cost to virtually everyone.

To see what is happening to, through, and around the category of democracy as it moves from Europe and North America into other continents, it is necessary to recognize not only what governmental forms or sequences of experience it is taken to refer to, but also what forms of equality it is heard to threaten or promise, and what types of economic structure are seen to be compatible with it or precluded by it. Everywhere that it now reaches has sooner or later to learn how to answer those questions through its own framework of understanding, on the basis of its own political and economic experience, and with its own immediate predicament in the forefront of its mind. The resulting political process is always extraordinarily complicated. There are brief passages of specious clarity in which the problems of mutual intelligibility apparently drop away and one regime form collapses, with another and plainly superior briskly replacing it (the Orange Revolutions forming perhaps the most prominent recent example). But it never takes long for intrinsic interpretive complexity to reassert itself and for the fog banks to roll back in and cut political visibility down to size. That cognitive constriction is not an intellectual failure of the present membership of our species (or professions), which might in principle be remedied by future enhancements of our performance. It is an ontological feature of the world, given by where and what we are, and we cannot hope to move briskly beyond it. What we can (and must) try to do is to learn to live with it with better grace and mutual forbearance.

To foster that forbearance, it is salutary to focus on one of the great historic regime collapses and reconstructions on other continents, which has reshaped the global structure of power over the past century. For most of that century, it would have been natural to begin with Russia; but the indisputable failure of that notable but clumsily conducted experiment, with the collapse of the USSR, has made the task of understanding why it took the course it did, or ended where it did, far less pressing, without making it any easier to discharge. At least for the present, it is more urgent to improve our grasp of what has been going on in the contrasting adventures of the category in two other great societies on the Asian landmass. In one of these, as part residue of Britain's Indian Empire, the category has been interpreted primarily in response to the political conduct and heritage of the former imperial power, if admittedly with later and not overwhelmingly instructive supplementation from Russia and China. In that setting, the category of democracy has been interpreted over time with close and insistent attention and great imaginative dynamism. In the other, China, encounter with democracy as a practical feature of the political world from the outset prompted more attention to America's idiosyncratic political experience.

By great good fortune, one of the subtlest and most illuminating accounts of the process through which the rest of the world has had to try to fathom the promise and menace lurking in this obtrusively Western category is provided in an essay by the Chinese scholar Xiong Yuezhi, which summarizes work he has undertaken over several decades.[20] It focuses on the inherent difficulties faced by Chinese officials, scholars, and journalists when they first tried to grasp what American democracy was, and on the closely connected difficulties that foreign missionaries or journalists also encountered when they too tried to convey their own understandings of its practical character and self-interpretation to Chinese readers or audiences. Some of these difficulties were essentially difficulties of translation—in linking the words of one language elaborated to understand and operate one set of political practices in one kind of society to those of another language developed to articulate and enact a very different set of practices in a drastically different kind of society. In the Chinese case, as the most talented interpreters of China's modern intellectual history have long demonstrated with great finesse,[21] the language into which the translation had to be made was peculiarly ill-suited to registering the point and character of barbarian political practices because it had come to be so heavily impacted on a millennially reiterated and consolidated vision of the political preconditions for civilization itself. The order of China's celestial empire was implacably hierarchical. It privileged peace and obedience to a single apex of authority; viewed conflict, dissidence, and still more active resistance with acute suspicion (at least until they had receded a tactful distance into the past); and saw the order it promised and aspired to provide as resting principally on the commitment and insight not merely of the emperors themselves and the personnel of the court through which they exercised their sway, but also of the scholar-officials and cultivated gentry throughout the provinces who largely sustained them and aspired to refine and edify their judgment.[22]

When the denizens of this highly differentiated and sometimes strongly intellectually engaged milieu first took up the challenge of attempting to comprehend barbarian political practices, their eye was firmly on power—on the peremptory need to turn the tables on the ever more intrusive, graceless, and disruptive traders and gunboats from the West. They sought to grasp where the power that was relentlessly molesting them had come from and what it rested on in order to draw on its sources for themselves. Since the agencies that menaced them themselves had only the haziest comprehension of the answer, it was bound to prove a lengthy and disconcerting quest. Even after the Chinese Communist Party's triumphal assumption of power in

1949, it remains far from clear how much real progress in ascertaining an answer had been made in China until Deng Xiaoping's decisive intervention.[23] Even then, the answer he hit upon was explicitly pragmatic, and agnostic over issues of political, economic, or cultural choice—any style of cat, provided that it catches the mice.[24]

If you inspect the current battlefront in that very long-running war of position, the role of democracy is very striking. To American observers, all but inevitably, it is a category that challenges the political standing of the Chinese Communist Party and the legitimacy of all who have risen to power through it. It hovers permanently on the brink of repudiating Chinese sovereignty over Taiwan, over Tibet, over Xinjiang, and if the People's Republic ever runs into big trouble and regional warlording recommences, potentially over any substantial segment of the country. From the viewpoint of China's rulers, it is a summons to revolution, to anarchy, or at very least to a dissipation or rupture of the power so triumphantly accumulated since 1979. To associates of the incumbent government, it is a category to which they have already taken the precaution of helping themselves. Whose republic is it, after all, if not the "People's"? Deployed by their foreign critics, or by state enemies, it indicts them for fraud or wrongful possession of what was never rightfully theirs.

This is clearly a disagreement about very many things. It ranges far and wide, evokes considerable animosity, and implicates pressing interests on both sides (though perhaps clearer and less readily admissible strictly personal stakes on the Chinese side: Whose republic is it indeed?). At a minimum, it is a disagreement about how it is appropriate for a society to acquire its leaders, how far those leaders should be subsequently left unimpeded to act as they choose, what effects the degree of discretion open to them in acting out their roles are likely to have on the scruples or self-restraint with which they choose to do so, and what effect the presence or absence of external scrutiny and personal accountability can be expected to exert on the benign or maleficent impact of their governing on those at the receiving end. These are a lot of issues to seek to organize through a single and somewhat nebulous concept; and it is scarcely surprising that the resulting disputes often prove dialogues of the deaf and virtually never much clarify the viewpoints of either party.

You can see that plurality of issues either analytically or politically. Viewed analytically, it remains intractably plural, and any political comprehension it contrives to provide is necessarily provisional and hypothetical, a kaleidoscope that shifts its patterns every time you alter the angle at which you hold it. Seen politically, it can of course be every bit as plural, and explicitly relative to the position and engagements of the individual or group that happens to be viewing it. But when it is viewed politically, it can also be summative, a judgment or choice, above all, about where the weight of a regime's political credibility does or should rest. It is over this last assessment that not only America's leaders but most of its politically interested population are so deeply at odds, not just with China's current political leaders, but also, as far we can currently ascertain, with most of China's politically interested population too. (Remember the anticipated response of Iraq's population to being rescued by "Shock and Awe.") The American conviction, which now seems to reach back uninterruptedly to 1776, comes above all from a process: the manner through which America's leaders come by their authority.

No one inspecting the United States today could sanely conclude that it is governed by its people; but a handsome majority of those who do in some sense govern it today, as throughout that impressive time span, have obtained or retained the opportunity to do so, whether directly or by delegation, by courtesy of the people. That is not a claim that can be defended for China at any point in its vastly longer history. Across the stark and sometimes violent disagreements over what the people have authorized or should authorize it to do, and however squalid, confused, and misguided they believe that sequence of choosing to have been, Americans stand more or less united in the proud conviction that any authority their own government has ever possessed to do anything has come to it through the free choice of the people. From the confidence and serenity of that viewpoint, it is hard for Americans, through all their domestic fears, humiliations, crimes, and sufferings, not to view the political predicaments of most of the world with some degree of condescension. Nothing infuriates the people of China more, across all their brutal political and personal inequalities, than what they see as barbarian condescension. Hence the feebleness of the impulse simply to accept as a unique and decisive validation a criterion of conspicuously barbarian provenance—the Chinese are not going to be reconciled to anything by news from pre-Confucian Mesopotamia[25]—and one that fetishizes a process through which those who currently rule have plainly not obtained their own opportunity to do so. Evidently enough, the implied relative evaluation of the standing of the respective states could hardly be acceptable to China's current rulers. But it is just as important to recognize the oddity, through the prism of China's vastly lengthier political experience,[26] of this entire way of conceiving the relative strengths and weaknesses of the two regimes.

It is not as yet plausible from the outside to suppose that China's experience may somehow secrete within it a conception of the responsibilities and character of the modern state that is potentially sounder and more powerful than the one that eventually emerged from Europe's largely self-inflicted political torments. But humans are a very intellectually inventive species, and it would be ill-advised (as well as impolite) to rule out the possibility in advance. But if Chinese political construals are unlikely to offer a superior wholesale replacement for American political understanding soon, it is far less evident that they do not already contain elements that might help to balance the latter and reframe contemporary judgments about what is to be done by whom across the world in a less unpromising fashion.

The American critique of China's present state, always latent though not always clearly audible in public or even private dialogue between the two, can be summarized simply. China's rulers have come by their authority through a process that could not stand inspection, that provides no clear or reliable restraints on how they deploy that authority, that leaves them minimally and whimsically accountable personally and wholly unaccountable corporately to those over whom they exercise it, that furnishes them with no predictably potent or edifying grounds to exert it with due consideration for the interests of those whom they rule, that fails with any consistency to equip them with the understanding or information required to recognize what those interests really are, and that therefore comprehensively fails to protect their subjects (China's alleged citizens) against the full impact of their indiscretion, cynicism, or stoniness of heart. A shade less confidently, quite a lot less plausibly, but also mercifully somewhat more mutedly, it goes on to suggest that these incumbents have proved very poor custodians of the interests of those whom they rule, and by implication far worse custodians than their American counterparts have contrived to prove themselves in the altogether seemlier and better-conceived political architecture in which history has privileged them to operate. It is important to think through to this last point in the analytical sequence, because it brings out the lack of balance in America's perspective on China and the consequent potential gain of rebalancing American political comprehension by what it is reasonable to think of as Chinese political comprehension (if in no sense a style of comprehension exclusive to China).

Until that final point in the analytic sequence, by necessity a moment of summation, there is no mistaking the force of the American critique of China's existing state. Indeed, you can pick up most elements in it sooner or later in more sporadic and dispersed fashion in the Chinese state's own discourse with itself and with its own subjects. A state of which all those charges hold good (and many have been implicitly acknowledged at intervals even by the state's own custodians and champions) is manifestly not a well-ordered state in good political health. Very plausibly, it is an ill-ordered state in a fairly advanced degree of corruption. And yet it is that state that has changed China more drastically than any previous state has ever changed the life chances of populations of distantly comparable size at anything like that pace. Much appalling harm has been perpetrated over those three decades; but there can hardly be a sane person in the world who could honorably will for China to turn the clock back to 1979. How much better in the round is the United States today as a habitat for its own citizens than it was in 1979, and for just which of them is it clearly better on balance? Democracy in the American understanding is no talisman for ensuring satisfactory political outcomes. It is as imprudent as it is wrong to offer it to others as though it were.

A balanced assessment of the relative merits of two very different societies' political arrangements is a precarious and taxing undertaking at the best of times, but as political experience globalizes uncontrollably, it is going to have to be undertaken more and more frequently and with ever growing urgency. Where the two societies in question are already incipiently vying for world power, and each can only view itself as the consummation of a long proud history or jeopardize its sense of identity by acknowledging irreparable hiatuses within that history, the intrinsic difficulty of the comparison itself is painfully exacerbated. To recognize China's formidable political strengths is already to begin to impugn America's political self-assurance, a step that is relatively effortless for China's own rulers and that many have quite audibly taken. For China's current rulers, whatever they feel about one another personally, they are corporately the source and basis of whatever order exists in and across China. There is no independent surviving source of order and no external basis on which they or anyone else could readily set out to construct one. To choose to jeopardize that already highly imperfect and conspicuously vulnerable order would be, in the classic phrase of Edmund Burke, "to play a most desperate game."[27]

What could give China's present rulers sufficient reason to embark upon that game? More pressingly, what *should* give them such a reason? Hardly the imperative to treat their own subjects better or enhance their net welfare as effectively as they can, duties they in effect fully acknowledge already in the breach, if not in the observance, and which they can only coherently hope to address by focusing and deepening the power of the state they currently head.

When Chinese officials or scholar-gentry first attempted to grasp what American democracy was, over a century and a half ago, they focused in turn on three questions: What exactly was the apex of the

American state? How did it get there and what kept it there? And what effects on the ways it subsequently acted did the way in which it got there really exert? It was the last of these three (the predictable effects of the mechanisms for attaining political power) that first attracted serious Chinese appreciation, but it did so at a point when there was no realistic possibility of China adopting the same model. In the lengthy interval since, none of these questions has lost interest, and all three have gained in apparent significance from America's rise to world power. Now, as then, the answers to the first two questions exerted little competitive pressure on Chinese visions of the basis and value of China's order.

The answer to the third question, by contrast, very soon began to press hard on these visions. It is the political configuration that emerged from that comparison which is the key to the political challenge America's democracy now poses to the legitimacy of China's state, and the corresponding solace that the American and Indian states each now draws from the common element in their own authorization. It would be foolish not to recognize how little competitive pressure China's rulers or their subjects yet feel from the answers to those first two questions, for all the main troubles and deformities that haunt their exercise of power. But its weight still depends on the relative feebleness of its challenge in those first two respects: its increasing failure to offer a convincing focus of authority, and its hazy relation to a past that any foreign population can readily imagine behind it.[28]

The American Dream has exerted astonishing power over a large and extravagantly variegated population across an impressive arc of time. Since Tocqueville and Beaumont returned from their historic visit,[29] news of that power has reached an ever wider audience across the world. But the power of the dream itself has traveled far less readily. To others in lands at varying distances away, the power held and exerted by the United States has usually seemed very different. It has looked and felt far less mesmerizing and often also quite menacing. As in the classic security dilemma between states, where it is hard to augment your own state's security without seeming to jeopardize that of others and so reinforce their reasons for raising their own capacity to threaten, every nation's pride in its own exemplary force presses naggingly on that of its fellows, forcing on them a defiant assertion of their own unique excellences and a demand for due deference and humility on the part of every other in face of these. America's confrontation with the erstwhile Third World was uneasy almost from the start for just this reason. In the face of China's remarkable ascent since 1979,[30] it has reached a new threshold of pain and danger.

THREE

Recognizing Democracy's Disorientation

It is still hard to bring into focus the key elements, intellectual as much as political, of the momentous confrontation between these two formidable regimes—the United States and China. On one side, that of the United States, it is a view of how governmental power can and should be built, authorized and directed across the countries of the world—call it "democracy"—along with a relaxed confidence that that view corresponds in very large measure to the way in which power has been built, authorized, and directed within its own territories and for its own people for an enviably long time. What that view highlights is the authorizing potential of a process of electoral competition, operating within a distinctive structure of inhibition and delay. The resulting model is very far from transparent, and it has operated in very different ways over time. What is clear from anywhere else in the world is that it casts very little light on how the power of the American state was in fact built, or the wealth of the American people created, and virtually none on how any as yet less fortunate population can reasonably hope to build the power of a state of their own, let alone augment their personal and collective wealth. Seen from elsewhere, the American vision of democracy appears to mistake a largely mythical picture of the genesis of American power with an unconnected and implausible recipe for generating a counterpower of its own.

On the other side of this confrontation, in China, there is a rueful awareness of how governmental power was in fact built in its own case, a more comforting sense of how effectively that power has by now been directed for a good three decades, and of the massive increments in wealth and military and diplomatic potency that have flowed from its direction, as well as an altogether more discomfiting sense of the flimsiness of its authorization by anything prior to and independent of its own recent success. There was, to be sure, the decisive Communist victory in China's long and brutal Civil War. But that was now some little time ago. Looking across the Taiwan Strait today, decades after Mao's great famine,[1] that confrontation now looks far more equivocal and more reductively military in character. For a relatively long time, in the face of the rest of the globe, the United States has reveled in its own wealth and power. It has felt no need to go in quest of either. The position of China's rulers could scarcely be more different. The authorization they now enjoy issues overwhelmingly from the spectacular scale of their all-too-recent success in finding and securing both. With the United States, prosperity, power, and authorization have gone hand in hand and done so almost from its outset. Many of its local ideologues are still strongly tempted to attribute America's power to its prosperity, and each in turn to the felicity of its secular authorization.

No minimally informed interpreter of China's experience could conceivably see it that way. In China, authorization remains a dimension of real jeopardy for the regime as a whole. Many assume, with varying assurance, that this conspicuous jeopardy is sure to prove inconsequential in practice, and if it does prove so, if economic momentum at its current velocity will authorize anything and might run on for ever, China's encounters with democracy as a word or an idea may prove to carry no residual political significance. The Communist Party's invocation of Lenin's intellectual aftermath, however anachronistic at other latitudes and however jejune in rational content, may continue to endow it with all the authorization it requires.[2] But it remains far from clear that that judgment will prove right. Authorization by momentum alone is notably hazardous for any regime. As soon as that momentum falters, the more squalid and brutal aspects of the basis on which it has been sustained come into sharper focus and the appeal to other bases of identification becomes costlier to dispense with. Under these circumstances, authorization by process gains sharply in appeal, and even a term like *democracy*, successfully neutered by decades of all but vacuous utilization, may alter brusquely in valency. There have been leading Chinese thinkers, some of them deeply influenced by the eminently American figure of John Dewey,[3] who have seen democracy in an essentially American understanding, as a recipe for China's political future; but they have not on the whole been lucky in their dealings with political power. (You could, I suppose, say much the same of Dewey himself.)[4] The attractions of Dewey's vision of democracy are above all its picture of a society flourishing through the active exertion and interactive intellectual energy of all its participants, a society surging with life and intelligence and constantly assailing the practical problems that come its way with all the human resources to hand. That picture assumes a society to be there in the first place, and there *as* a society, an assemblage of human beings already capable of recognizing one another's social membership and acting with, as well as against, one another. It assumes a potential order not grounded on the coercion of some by others, and assumes that what is there independently of coercion isn't just the state of nature.

The Chinese picture, in all its historical heterogeneity, assumes something very different. It assumes that if order is to be present in human life, its character and content must be recognized intellectually and constructed and secured in practice by the will, judgment, and persuasive capabilities of those who are able to recognize it. It assumes the need to teach the principles of order to those without the personal discernment to recognize them for themselves, and assumes the need to convey to those who cannot be trusted to do the discerning for themselves the imperative to accept its being done for them by those who can. If the American vision of justified authority is horizontal and heuristic, a process of discovery between those on much the same level, its Chinese counterpart, with all due variation over the bewilderingly long time that it has been deployed, is hierarchical and didactic.[5] It assumes both the need for and the potential availability of a definite apex of authority, and one that can and should force its superior insight on the rest of its fellow Chinese and, still more over the last two centuries, on the fellow citizens with the misfortune not to have been born Han Chinese.

It is very difficult to think across these two spaces with any clarity and see how each bears on the other. It is also lethally prejudicial to any attempt to do so to assume that either space offers a privileged perspective from which to try to make that attempt. The single most important point about the significance of democracy's odyssey as a political formula is the intellectual absurdity and political menace of trying to grasp it, of all political phenomena, on the basis of any such privilege.

But what is the alternative? How can anyone think of anything except from his or her own point of view? The late Samuel P. Huntington incurred great contumely (as well as coming into a handsome income stream) for insisting that civilizations have always clashed throughout human history and were rather evidently continuing to do so even today.[6] The abuse heaped on him for this relatively commonplace observation was distributed fairly evenly across the presumed motives that led him to make his claim, the political damage critics saw his insistence as certain to inflict, and the intellectually uncouth mode of thinking with which they saw him as developing his train of thought.

Democracy's odyssey, unprecedented in the history of human speech, is an object lesson in how to register the weight of the phenomena that Huntington invoked, without succumbing to either the fatalism or the chauvinism his critics hastened to ascribe to him. As democracy at long last carries its exhilarations and vulnerabilities forward across the frontier that most preoccupied him—the demographic or political boundaries of the community of Islam across the world—it is easier to see clearly what that passage does and does not mean. The inspirational surge of democracy across that frontier did not come from somewhere else. It had been there, in bitter waiting and little, if any, hope for a very long time.

The primal appeal and force of democracy in the form in which it has survived into the modern world lies in that moment of rejection. It is when the people declare, as they did in the squares of Tunis and then of Cairo, Benghazi, and even Damascus, that what they do not want is the regime itself. In those settings, however discrepant the reasons that have brought the challengers together, and however incompatible many of the purposes that between them they hope to realize, often what becomes hypnotically concrete is what they are choosing to reject. In that, if in very little else, the purpose that brings them together and the outcome they mean to achieve is as focused, as unitary, and even as fleetingly solidary as the political purposes of people in very large numbers ever get. For the present, however temporarily, the option against the regime is in the first place the option for democracy, because democracy in vaguest outline is just the default option. Either the regime or democracy or chaos. Most people in downtown Cairo, Tripoli, or Damascus, as much as anywhere else, want chaos least of all.[7] Almost none can afford it except very briefly indeed. So what they want is either the regime or something unmistakably different; and for the present, the name for the unmistakably different is democracy: the political form of whatever the people, when permitted to choose, in due course prove to want instead.

Contrast this with the picture of democracy's arrival anywhere, as it is natural for Americans to see this, and as some of them at least did see it for a few years after 1989. "In the beginning," said John Locke very long ago, espousing a rather different ideological agenda, "all the world was America."[8] More than three centuries later, for democracy to have become the default option in regime change seemed very briefly to presage a striking global destination. In the end, at least politically, all the world might become America: American in its political tastes, American in its political habits, and hence American also in its ultimate allegiances. But that is scarcely what it ever could have meant for democracy to cross any frontier at all. Very much like autocracy, democracy is a self-indigenizing category. As it crosses any frontier, both by conceptual necessity and by eminently practical causality, democracy takes on the coloring of the population to which it comes. Its boast is to reflect the tastes and the choices of that population; and sooner or later, unless it is thrust back again and expelled beyond the border, reflect them it will. The politics of Gaza are remarkably grim; but for Hamas to win its key election was not a derogation from democracy. It was what democracy, in all its dedicated aberration of judgment, imperatively required at that point.

It is easiest for most of us to see the impediments to mutual understanding when others are attempting to understand us than when we strain to understand them. When Chinese officials first attempted to take in the nature of America's regime, as Xiong Yuezhi makes clear, they certainly did not set out from the idea of democracy.[9] Instead, they began with the question of what lay at the apex of the American state: the fact that America lacked a monarch and had to make do with a mere headman instead. As the governor-general of Liang-Guang Province (now Guangdong and Guangxi) reported to the imperial court in 1817, in response to the opium smuggled in on American ships, these particular

> barbarians have no monarch whatsoever, only a headman. The tribe publicly selects several men, who serve in succession according to the drawing of lots, for terms of four years apiece. Commercial affairs are managed independently by private individuals who are not controlled or deputed by the headman.[10]

Two decades later, in an unsigned article on the United States of North America in the missionary-edited *Eastern Western Monthly Magazine*, the author reported that "The people rule the country themselves, and once every three years elect a leader to manage governmental affairs."[11] The following year a more expansive article in the same periodical reported once more that the Americans did not set up a king as ruler of their country. Instead they

> selected a president (*tongling*), vice-president (*fu tongling*) and other high officials to serve four-year terms. The president must be attentive to the people's wishes, and have a deep understanding of the arts of statecraft, so as to implement benevolent governance. Thus the regulation of the entire realm hinges on this single pivot: the chief executive

> exercises control over his subordinate officials and thereby regulates the country's notables, he keeps the various affairs of government in order and thereby pacifies the common people.[12]

The overall picture may have overlapped a little with George Washington's, but by 1838 it was a deeply Chinese vision of what the American political process had become: keeping governmental affairs in order from above by controlling subordinate officials, regulating the notables, and thus pacifying the common people. Like the emperor, the president was the pivot of the entire system; and, as in China, the key object was to pacify the common people. What was already clear in this article, however, was that in America the common people took much more pacifying and maintained a far higher degree of surveillance of their ruler than was open to their Chinese counterparts. Both advantages and disadvantages of these arrangements were soon recognized even in China, and the office of president extricated from a vocabulary commonly employed to pick out village headmen, gunboat captains, or leaders of bandit gangs and elevated to a more suitably honorific status. Within half a century, interested Chinese had left behind them a degree of ignorance that could assimilate presidential choice to the outcome of a lottery (a more prejudicial verdict on the American approach to ordering governmental affairs than even Plato chose to pass on the whimsicality of Athenian political choice, despite the ideological centrality of random selection to the Athenian practice of political equality).[13] By this point, Chinese interpreters could readily recognize the weight of public opinion in shaping the agency of America's state. A century and three-quarters later, very large numbers of China's population know vastly more about America's recent political history. But the sheer imaginative difficulty of holding up one set of political arrangements against the other, and judging which looks best equipped to realize the political goods you value most highly, has not noticeably lessened for Chinese observers over time; and the prospective contribution of democracy is still likelier to feature as one element in that puzzle than as the basis for its solution. It is far from obvious that that judgment on the Chinese part is simply misplaced.

There is good reason to believe that the gap between American and Chinese visions of politics is wider than most such gaps between very large populations consciously aware of inhabiting the same world at the same time. It is a precondition for recognizing the scale of that gap to see that the gap itself is not simply the product of America's historical felicity and China's until very recently relative historical misfortune over most, if not all, of the historical existence of the United States. Still less is it a product of the exquisite political taste with which that fortunate history has endowed America's current citizens and the miserably depleted political imagination with which China's current inhabitants for the most part have to make do. A more adequate way to see what has produced it is to register two momentous and far less reassuring factors. In the first place, it is to take in the vastly greater historical depth of the Chinese vision and the consequent difficulty of reshaping it stably and decisively. China's modern historians, especially from the United States, have shown in vivid and fascinating detail just how hard it proved over the long, slow nineteenth century for China to let go of dynastic monarchy as a form of government, without consciously surrendering any sense of social value or political meaning at all.[14] In the second place, it is to acknowledge how miserably inadequate the West's intellectual resources for understanding politics have proved for China, as it struggled against the military and technical superiority, first of the Western powers and then of Japan, and the cumulatively disruptive penetration of China's economy, territory, and way of life from each direction. Even to concede the superiority of a republic over a dynastic monarchy was a very hard stretch and, as in the French case, initially open to prompt reconsideration. Finding a way in which a republic could be relied upon to cope with military threat, whether internal or external, proved impossible. The subordination of officials and the regulation of notables was scarcely even attempted; and the implementation of benevolent government lay all too evidently beyond reach.

When later and more ambitious offshoots of Western political thinking arrived via Russia and were suitably indigenized in their turn, China's luck scarcely improved.[15] The economic expedients recommended to China's new rulers by Russian advisers were not especially successful and have since been abandoned more or less in their entirety. Chinese improvisations in their place over the first three decades of Communist Party rule often failed to prove a clear improvement and have also mostly since been abandoned. The record in subordinating officials, regulating notables, and furnishing benevolent government was more checkered and harder to read; but it remains hard to attribute its more discouraging elements to the spurning of clear conceptions or reliable expedients of European or North American provenance for how to structure power or hold it to benign purposes, still less to ensure that its consequences are beneficial for the great majority of China's population.

But China's remarkable economic transformation over the past three decades has not been just a lucky accident. Neither China's long history nor the cumulative intellectual acumen of the West showed China's rulers how to do what they have in fact done. Under ferocious pressure and with remarkable audacity and nerve, they worked it out for themselves. They set and sustained a framework in which scores of millions of people reshaped an economic landscape at breakneck speed and tilted the economy of the world in a new direction. It is anyone's guess how long that transformation can go on with anything like its current momentum, or how far it can ever hope to repair the collateral damage it has inflicted along the way. But it has occurred. And the political choices and exertions of the political entity that still rules China made it possible for it to do so. That entity certainly has no avowable or compelling answer to the questions of why it should be ruling China or why it can reasonably be expected to rule it beneficently for the foreseeable future. What it does still have for the present is the "Mandate of Heaven."

In some respects, which its present leaders intermittently acknowledge (and others to which they understandably prefer to turn a blind eye), it has definitely not been ruling at all beneficently. But the people of China need China to be ruled; and like the people of everywhere else, they cannot at any particular moment pick and choose the structures through which they are being ruled or will be ruled for the near future. The one opportunity the people of America evidently have in that respect, and which the people of China conspicuously lack, is the opportunity to pick many of the personnel in the upper reaches of their state at regular intervals and, most strikingly of all, to pick the single individual at its apex. Unlike the emperor, who was picked at least conceptually by suprahuman forces, the people of America can pick their own headman (or, as it must be sooner or later, headwoman). For all the weight of frustration and disappointment that swirls around it, that option still has some imaginative centrality in American understandings of democracy and still retains its evanescent gratifications.

What is gratifying about it is not the predictable benefit (individual or collective) of the consequences of exercising it; it is the immediacy of personal choice itself. There is no reason whatever to suppose that China's citizens would not enjoy exercising that choice as much as any other citizens. But there is nothing in China's protracted prior history to give them grounds to believe that exercising their choice will prove a good recipe for ensuring that the headman selected will shape China's state agency for the best. When the Chinese first sought to fathom the American approach, quite early in the nineteenth century, some thought George Washington looked to be quite a good proxy for an emperor. But that was a very long time ago; and the vicissitudes of more recent presidents do not and should not suggest a comparable capacity to impart order to America's turbulent political processes. Leaving the choice of headman to the discernment of the people is not a strategy that instantly recommends itself in

Beijing. It is not a natural practical inference from China's millennial political history or the intellectual history so closely impacted upon it.

The last point needs such emphasis because the mutual political comprehension of China's and America's political elites matters so intensely at present. To gauge what it now means, it helps to compare America's bewilderments in the face of China with the challenge to mutual political intelligibility posed by another great Asian state, the Republic of India. If there are any democracies in the world today—if the term *democracy* is not simply a misnomer when applied to any extant state—the Republic of India is by far the largest democracy there has ever been. It is also in some ways the most surprising democracy there has ever been: surprising in its scale, in its persistence among a huge and, for most of its existence, still exceedingly poor population, and in its tensile strength in the face of fierce centrifugal pressures and high levels of violence, corruption, and human oppression throughout most of its existence.

Why is it still there as a continuous legal, political, organizational, and cultural structure? Why does it still cover its present territorial extension and continue to hold the huge human population that still lives upon this? Why is it still valued so highly by so many of its own citizens, miserably poor as much as enviably wealthy,[16] in the face of levels of corruption and criminality across its political class, which must be as high today as they have ever been since the republic's founding,[17] and levels of violence deeply embedded in its social and religious relations, which even six decades of purposefully remedial constitutional rule and any number of elaborate programs of legal, economic, and social reform have largely failed to pacify? It is hard to exaggerate the importance of the fact that it is still there. It is also hard to imagine what democracy's future would look like if the republic had continued to disintegrate in the wake of the initial partitioning of Britain's Indian Empire—the Partition of India as it then was—or even if the residue of that empire had in due course gone the way of Pakistan. The sheer fact of that survival has shown two things very clearly: the extraordinary absorptive capacity of democracy as a political category, and its severely limited capacity to impose order on chaos and the muted inclination even to attempt to do so. If there is inspiration in its tumultuous journey, as there unmistakably is, there is also at least equivalent chastening: high romance alongside very grim realism. Far the best portrait of this trajectory so far, with the steadiest balance between realism and romance, is Ramachandra Guha's wonderfully generous and unconcessive history, *India After Gandhi*.

What has made it possible for India's republic to last for more than six full decades is a number of elements in its legacy from British imperial rule and from the lengthy and profound struggles to escape from that rule.[18] The principal legacy from imperial rule itself was essentially common to the two initial successor states, but the legacy from the struggles against it was distributed altogether less symmetrically. It is tempting, accordingly, especially for Indians, to attribute the divergence in democracy's fortunes in these two states to the weaker and less edifying political resources of Jinnah's Muslim League and to the cumulative nationalist achievement of the Congress Party and its great leaders, especially, in their very different ways, to Mohandas Gandhi, Jawaharlal Nehru, and Vallabhbhai Patel. The record of India's subsequent political leaders has been both more checkered and more ordinary, though it has certainly encompassed at intervals very considerable personal achievements, and at least one of them, for better and for worse, was a very notable political leader indeed. But what stands out with the benefit of hindsight is how singularly fortunate India's republic was in its founders,[19] in the imaginative scale and intensity Gandhi had given to the quest for nationhood across so many scores of millions of people before nationhood was won,[20] the vision, patience, and political courage of Nehru in defining sovereign nationhood as he went along,[21] and the massive political realism and good sense of Patel when the time came to assume it. It was a great political feat to turn the scruffy palimpsest of empire into a cohesive territorial state in relatively steady control, over most of its subsequent history, of borders that were often intensely vulnerable both from the outside and from within. It was a great political feat to recreate even a semblance of civic order across most of that territory through the grim and bloody aftermath of Partition and to recompose it time and again in the face of decades of bitter economic, caste, and communal conflict in an endless variety of settings. There was no overriding reason why India should not have split and resplit endlessly through one secession after another, as may yet happen with Pakistan, and as began to do so decades ago with the creation of Bangladesh.

The reason why India did not go that way is not well focused even today. It is in part certainly a consequence of the scale and character of the Indian army, and the pride that it has contrived to sustain, in the face of pressing personal temptations, in placing the constitutional integrity of the state above the gratification of individual ambition and corporate self-advancement. It is in part a product of the prodigious administrative reach of the Indian state, for all its bureaucratic clumsiness and rigidity and its fluctuating commitment to legal responsibilities—a reach most evocatively shown in the stunning complexity and punctiliousness of its electoral rituals and the unique political standing of their emblematic institution, the Election Commission of India. It is certainly in part also a product of the depth of thought-through political construction embodied in its constitution-making,[22] and the stamp that placed on the continuing project of a rule of law that might readily have been vitiated irretrievably by its imperial provenance or by cynical deflection into the subsequent convenience of a varyingly beleaguered or appropriative executive.

Within the frame of India's republic, these resources have to a striking degree worked together and not, as they quite readily might have done and have necessarily in fact done from occasion to occasion, worked more or less lethally against one another. There have been times of great peril in enabling them to do so—notably the period of Indira Gandhi's Emergency, but also with Partition right at the beginning, recurrently with Jammu and Kashmir, with the traumas of Amritsar, the poison flooding out from Ayodhya, the endless miseries of Bihar, and the hapless rural backlands, which have subsequently succeeded to its mantle, and the Marathi nationalist outrages in Mumbai and Gujarat.

You can also question the felicity of their consequences: Ask how far they have worked to the net benefit of a very large proportion of India's population at any point in its history, and also question equally, as you can in any capitalist democracy, how far such benefits, as have accrued from their working for that huge population, have been augmented or depleted by the operations more specifically of India's democratic institutions. If the latter had worked very substantially worse, it is reasonable to assume that that would have very substantially impaired the appeals of these institutions; and no doubt if their consequences for the wealth and standard of living of a clear majority had been very much handsomer, that too would have ingratiated democracy as a political principle to more of India's citizens. But if you tried to trace out systematically how these consequences have in fact accrued, their net impact would be hard to read. Since its Athenian heyday, democracy has had more flair and animus when it comes to distribution than when it comes to production. Some of the distributive gains of the conspicuously badly off in given settings have been traceable unequivocally to the democratic bargaining within Indian political institutions and to explicitly articulated rectificatory purposes. In these respects it is hard to see how democratic institutions could vindicate themselves more conclusively. The long slow struggle to offset the accumulated historical oppression of the lower castes, untouchables, and tribals with the spiritual authority of Gandhi behind it, and the shaping impact of B. R. Ambedkar, both in the drafting of the constitution itself and throughout his long political career, driving it forward, certainly generated anomalies of its own along the way; but it too has been as serried and admirable a project of rectifying a vast historical injustice as human history can plausibly point to. In it too, democracy has carried a large proportion of the burden; and if it is scarcely to India's credit as a civilizational site (let alone to the credit of the British Empire) that the new republic inherited so much to rectify, it is hard to think of an attributable outcome of democracy in operation that is so unequivocally to its credit.

For all the often deeply unpleasant cautionary tales that disfigure it, the record of India's democracy as a whole forms a single giant political achievement and one that has already had an immense impact on the political imaginations of other countries and may yet have very much more. If we press the question of why that achievement has been effected, besides the historical legacies that made it possible and the wide range of political actions through which it was reached and secured, there is something else left over that is central to the theme I have been trying to explore: the special Indian engagement with democracy as a category, and the wealth and heterogeneity of the potential that Indians have elicited from their romance with it and their explorations of it.

That theme should carry a special resonance for an American audience, both for the opportunity it offers for widening imaginative sympathy and for the instructive complement it provides to America's own rather different romance with and exploration of the category. The Indian tale, as yet, has been told even more fitfully and less illuminatingly than the American, if for somewhat different reasons. But this protracted inaudibility from the outside (and in part even within India itself) is beginning at last to come to an end, and the story of India's political thinking from the twentieth century onward is now being told with increasing confidence and intimacy as a cumulative record of political experience and even political learning. It has yet to be joined convincingly to an understanding of India's long intellectual past, the cumulative riches especially of classical Sanskrit learning and the proliferation of vernaculars across the subcontinent.[23] But joined in due course it is going to be; and when it is, there is no reason why India's dramatic political experience should look (or feel) any less coherent than the political experience of America or France, Britain or Germany, Japan or, dare one say it, China itself. And in India's political experience, whatever will be true by then for Japan or China, or indeed Germany or Britain, neither of whose experiences still appears especially exemplary, democracy will certainly still have become the master category. It isn't just that India's national elections, each time they occur, are always the biggest democratic elections there have ever been; it is also that democracy's adventure in India is still the greatest adventure on which that endlessly untransparent category has yet to launch itself.

You can see that adventure from several different angles—at a minimum, intellectual, organizational, heuristic, and coercive. To do it any justice you must at least try to see it in each of those ways and then put its different trajectories across each of them together. Especially you must do so if you hope to extricate your own understanding of democracy from the necessarily parochial framing in which you will inevitably have formed it. On the Indian subcontinent, and particularly since independence in India itself, more women and men have peered into democracy's mirror and strained to take in what they see than have done so anywhere else. True, initially, they did so on a more modest scale than the immigrant population of the United States has chosen to over the last two or three centuries. It is a safe bet that the term *democracy* cannot be shown to have reached India before the eighteenth century at the earliest. But it remains a very deep question how far the idea and practice of democracy had featured in the texture of Indian society and the workings of Indian imaginations as far back as, or even farther than, it can plausibly be seen to appear in any European society. Just how that immemorial if shadowy presence was to relate to, inform, and constrain India's destiny and capabilities as an independent state was a central issue of judgment and allegiance for the nationalist movement from quite early in the twentieth century. It very much remains such, however confusedly, as the society as a whole faces its future today.

You can think of the presence of democracy in India simply as the current form of its state. But you can also think of it, and may do so with greater sympathy as many Indians emphatically do, as the diffuse set of practices, elaborately dispersed across the social landscape, that make up India's civil society at all levels, from villages to political or commercial capitals, endlessly reinserting itself between government and individual citizens and tussling away to soften coercive impacts on those worst placed to defend themselves and to buoy up the facilities to support those most abjectly in need (as well, undoubtedly, as pursuing a prodigious variety of other and far less edifying goals). It is easy for denizens of each of those settings—rulers and activists alike—to view their mutual relation in zero-sum terms, as a ceaseless struggle for dominance. But it defies the sense of democracy, either as a term or as an idea, to see their relation that way. In each setting and from each angle, the demos (or the group who fondly identifies itself with its interests and, hence, with it too) judges or acts as best it can on its behalf and with its presumptive authority. No one who disapproves of what he or she chooses to do is likely to view this more charitably because of the authority it invokes. But whatever facilities it may offer for self-deception, or whatever abuses it can cynically be put to, you cannot reasonably deny that the category of democracy is open to both interpretations, and that something of normative and political significance and value is captured in each. To misapply a political category is never to invalidate it. There are no political concepts or categories capable of carrying validity that cannot also be more or less grossly misapplied. One of the lessons we most urgently need to learn about democracy is how readily and unresistingly it can be misapplied, and how practically contradictory even perfectly defensible applications of it can readily prove. That is why the experience of democracy was always bound to prove such a maze, and why anyone who hopes to see the politics of any democratic polity clearly must learn to look beyond the category itself.

Viewing democracy's adventure in India as a highly populated passage of intellectual history, there are several different sequences to attend to, and an increasingly crowded canvas as you move toward the present and try to peer forward beyond it. Two in particular can be traced in exemplary fashion in the work of Karuna Mantena, and especially in her fine study *Alibis of Empire*. The first, the inherent contradictions of liberal imperialism, was at first an occidental intrusion—an aspiring remedy for the blatantly untoward profile of unapologetically preliberal imperialism, the long shadow of Warren Hastings, or at least of the specter of his rule passed on by Edmund Burke to Britain's political class. Liberal imperialism at all points was a project rather than a plausible historical description of governmental practice: imperial rule as a favor for those at the receiving end—humanitarian intervention for the very long haul. Its totemic exponent, John Stuart Mill, classic theorist of democracy as collective self-education for those he deemed up to it, firmly denied its applicability to pre-Habermasian social time—as Mill himself put it: "Any state of things anterior to the time when mankind have become capable of being improved by free and equal discussion."[24] He based his analysis firmly on the contrast between civilization and barbarism, with the former defined by "human beings acting together for common purposes in large bodies"[25] and fully capable of reciprocation and hence of rule following, and the latter briskly inverting the assessment and hence requiring "direct subjection by the more advanced."[26] Mill himself was serenely confident in the quality of his own intellectual and political judgment, seeing "the main point of superiority in the political theories of the present" as their acceptance that the institutions through which a population is ruled "need to be radically different according to the stage of advancement already reached,"[27] and taking his cue from his own father's precept that no "scheme of government can happily conduce to the end of government, unless it is adapted to the state of the people for whose use it is intended."[28]

It is easy today to sneer at Mill's complacency over the imperial element in the ways he and his father had chosen to spend their lives. It is hard, too, not to enjoy his merciless pillorying by James Fitzjames Stephen for the vision of Britain's Indian Empire as based on "a moral duty on the part of the English nation to try to educate the natives in such a way as to lead them to set up a democratic form of government administered by representative institutions," and to warm to Stephen's challenge why what was good enough for Charlemagne and Akbar in their emphatically coercive dealings with backward states of society should not carry through to the relations between the educated and uneducated back in Britain itself.[29]

But it is dangerous to sneer too readily. We have scarcely left the dilemmas of liberal imperialism comfortably behind us; and if we shrink from employing the criterion of advancement explicitly any longer, we direly need a less condescending proxy for its strictly pragmatic counterpart. What clear and reliable advances have we yet made in discerning how to enable failed states to succeed or to induce states without either capacity or inclination to civilize their subjects to set about the arduous struggle to do so? How much more robustly directive is our own theory of how to civilize the world than Mill's has proved to be? It is especially important to register that question since, however haphazardly and in the teeth of Stephen's sneer, there is a clear sense in which, by independence, Britain's Indian administrators had at least enabled enough Indians to educate themselves in such a way as led them to set up precisely "a democratic form of government administered by representative institutions." That form of government is still there today; and it was the clear choice in the end of the main strand in India's nationalist movement that it should be; and they made that choice, through very extensive argument and often bitter conflict, over quite a long time. That is the third of the sequences you would need to trace, as intellectual history, to grasp the full impact of democracy on India. As I have already tried to suggest, it has also proved the most momentous. Even with the privilege of hindsight, that option still comes out as India's largest strictly political resource in establishing and sustaining the most astonishing democracy there has yet been.

It is the second sequence on which Mantena has concentrated most of her work thus far.[30] She begins from a deep intellectual reaction to John Stuart Mill's viewpoint, prompted in large part by dismay at the evident fragility of imperial rule in the wake of the 1857 uprising, a favor flamboyantly unrecognized as such by its recipients. The reaction pivoted on the intellectual work of Sir Henry Maine, who recast the vice-regal image of India and helped to transform much of the sophisticated European sense of what a society really consists in by doing so. He focused on India's innumerable villages and the complex practices that sustained them, saw in their beleaguered residual autonomy a balance between promise and danger, and set out to try to guide his imperial colleagues in the formidable assignment of shoring up the promise and controlling the danger.

Movingly, and for reasons we still do not clearly understand, Maine's remarkable reorientation of the imperial mind set up intricate resonances between European (and, in due course, American) efforts to rethink the modern state as an intricate and gratuitously overconfident pseudo-totality in necessarily and deservedly limited control of a burgeoning array of substate institutions, many of which had long preceded it and had distinctly better prospects of operating coherently from the point of view of their human participants. The European wing of this movement of thought, pluralism, did not itself, for the most part, set off from Maine. It came and then very largely went, over a few decades, though it has recently begun to seep back. Its American wing never encountered the same level of resistance from admirers or would-be deployers of the state and has remained a fairly steady presence throughout.[31]

But in India itself, in quite direct response to Maine and many of the realities of Indian society, pluralism figured dramatically in shaping the Swadeshi element in the nationalist movement, inspired a highly distinctive vision of India's realities and possibilities—centered on tilting power, initiative, and social hope back from state centers toward the villages—and generated some of the most striking imaginative moments in India's modern intellectual history, from Radhakamal Mookerji's Lucknow School of Sociology, and his 1923 study in comparative politics, *Democracies of the East*, to the mesmerizing figure of Mohandas Gandhi and the great champions of India's indefatigably still-burgeoning civil society from 1949 up to today. It also joined India's politics to the intricacies of its enduring religious heritage more richly and with more promise than the legions of electoral politicians who have traded on the claim to do so ever since the spoils of office came within reach.

It cannot be said that this remarkable inspiration has ever achieved a tight grip on the performance of its inveterate and often immediate enemy, the Indian state.

But that was a victory plainly precluded from the start. If it is scarcely facing a kinder ecology in the near future, as India's growth rate accelerates at last and its leading capitalists loom ever larger, it is also by now clear that the presence it has assumed across Indian society is too dense and pervasive for there to be any chance that its voice will simply die away.

The scale of democracy's impact on India raises pressing questions both for Indians themselves and for the rest of the world's inhabitants. For Indians, the most important judgment is how on balance that impact has come out. For the rest of us, the key question is what it shows about the political properties of democracy as a category and its capacity to survive and root itself in different settings and then direct the political energies of their inhabitants for the better. We can judge the answers to both questions best by pressing the question of what democracy has done and meant for Indians themselves. The criteria here are not elusive. How far has it aided and impeded them in their individual and collective quests for wealth and power? How successfully has it reconciled a society in which every adult member is deemed fully fit to judge and act politically for themselves to the dizzying injustice of so much of its own past, or aided it to recompose its totemic hierarchies of caste and its brutal chasms of class into a community of real equals?[32] How far in addressing each of these exacting (and arguably fantastical) goals has it equipped the citizens of India to recognize and respond to their ever more pressing need to preserve and restore a viable habitat in which to do so? How safely and securely has it woven these tasks together so that none disappears from sight or suffers irreparably from prioritizing the others? By those standards, has Indian democracy proved a good idea, or has it proved a strikingly bad one?

FOUR

Recovering Our Bearings

Fatality, Choice, and Comprehension

If democracy as we currently understand it reliably clarified political choices, and if it did thus give human populations a dependable means to orientate themselves in the real existential and biological settings of their lives, we would know by now, after more than six decades, whether Indian democracy has proved to be a good idea or a strikingly bad one. And even if many foreigners, for one reason or another, were still impeded in recognizing the answer to that question, we can be confident that the great majority of India's own population would be well aware what it is. As it happens, there is by now surprisingly good reason to believe that the latter is in fact true and that the answer is positive, if less than emphatic.[1]

Some of the blemishes in India's democracy have long been obvious enough: the speed and insouciance with which Indira Gandhi's Emergency was imposed; the continuing degradation of the living conditions and personal treatment of large segments of the untouchables and tribals; the openly cynical logrolling, which dominates so much of its routine politics; the flagrant corruption of a state apparatus, infinitely open on all too many channels to malignant intelligence, energy, and initiative; the clear deterioration in intellectual and moral quality of India's political class and its increasingly rampant criminality (so spectacularly at odds with the presuppositions of constitutional democracy); the brutality of its police force and often of its military practices in local repression; and the state's severely limited efficacy in policing itself.[2]

Unsurprisingly, the blemishes in India's democracy are at least as easy to identify from inside India as they could be from the outside. But viewed from the inside, they merge indiscernibly with the substance of India itself, as the idea of democracy, if it is not to be a travesty, in the last instance requires that it should. Democracy might have been a good or a bad idea for India when it won its independence. But India itself was neither a good nor a bad idea. (By now you could not confidently say the same for Pakistan, which was quite a definite political idea at the time and has since not worn well as such.) At that point India itself cannot illuminatingly be said to have been an idea at all. Rather, like every other human society, it was a palimpsest of historical achievement, failure, and mishap and an unfathomable human predicament. Among the questions that faced it at that point was whether or not to become a constitutional democracy. It is from the subsequent fortunes of its answer to that question that the world as a whole can now learn something fresh and potentially dramatic about what democracy does and does not imply.

Some of what it can learn from India over this time span it could perfectly well learn from elsewhere. You can readily infer from most protracted experiences of representative democracy in action in capitalist settings that the formal political equality democracy promises and purports to guarantee is fully compatible with perpetuating devastating inequality and injustice. But even those inured to the scale of each in their own society may still be shocked by the heterogeneity and extremity of India's variations on that ancient human theme. More interestingly, if discontinuously and sometimes disconcertingly, you can also learn that the workings of constitutional democracy over many decades can in due course prove an effective and ingratiating palliative even to huge and deeply historically entrenched injustice. More pressingly still, you can learn that the long, slow, erratic, and ungainly recognition and amendment of historically profound injustice is a clearly superior alternative to political projects of erasing extreme injustice by frontal assault, like the killing fields of the Khmer Rouge (a lesson still pertinent to large areas of India's countryside). You can also draw more positive and enlivening inferences from the same experience. If democracy almost certainly will not over any time horizon eliminate extreme inequality and evident injustice from a capitalist world to which we have no sane alternative, we now know that it can be installed and durably sustained, with due historical luck, even in vast and miserably poor societies. On as large a scale as human political ideas have yet been tried out, extreme poverty does not preclude democracy.

Moreover, once it has been installed and for as long as it can be sustained, as Amartya Sen has long insisted,[3] it can lift a millennially grim threat from human populations, the threat of famine and mass starvation because of the maldistribution of potentially available food resources. What Bengal meant for the first half of the twentieth century, and Ireland for the century before, and what China alas meant for countless millions of its own citizens well after India's independence,[4] no democratic polity need ever mean again. We should not exaggerate the scope or reliability of this finding. It is unclear how far it rests on the structure of political authority itself and how far it has issued from the continuing independence from governmental control of India's newspaper press, an economic outcome as much as a legally guaranteed status, and an economic outcome scarcely guaranteed by the dynamics of any capitalist economy. But even read with all due caution and qualification, the record of India's democratic experience offers a luminous demonstration of what it is about this elusive idea that has given it such remarkable historical impetus over the last two centuries and a ringing vindication of its capacity to benefit the human populations that take it up.

It is, though, still as essential as ever not to mistake what that capacity implies. To perform well over time, a political order has above all to muster and sustain authority and to direct the judgment of those who hold it to act effectively for the better. Not all human populations are in a position to do that within any conceivable political framework. Nothing at this point can be offered in good faith to the suffering people of Somalia (still less effectively provided) that could predictably serve them for these purposes; and it seems at best unlikely that anyone has yet seen how to provide it to the inhabitants of Afghanistan or the Democratic Republic of the Congo or the bitterly divided population of Libya. History can be brutal to human populations and often conspicuously remains so. In a far wider range of settings than anyone seriously surmised three centuries ago, democracy in variants of its modern format may well be accessible through resources historically available to the societies that are already there. But it is no magical device to conjure up those resources where they are grimly absent. The dilemmas of liberal imperialism have not faded from the world. A richer, better armed, and technically more advanced society is no guarantee of a kinder or more discerning one.

Democracy has not proved a dependable heuristic for a latent normative order in any society we know, even where there may have been such an order there to discern in the first place. The experience of India confirms this less than startling finding as amply as that of the United States or France, Britain or Germany, Ireland or Greece. But however undependable a mechanism it remains for judging what to do in the end, in India as everywhere else, India's independent experience has established democracy's unique dynamism as a heuristic for the full range of social purpose, sentiment, and aspiration present in it as buoyantly as America's did for Tocqueville.[5] Democracy has given rise to and fomented the seething biological vitality and the insistent proliferation of India's efflorescent civil society. Often it has given that multifarious and elusive social reality little purchase on the content or outcomes of state decisions; but throughout it has obstructed a very great deal of what that state would otherwise have had a mind to do, and opened up the penetralia of India's bewilderingly complex society in a way no previous epoch in Indian history could conceivably have tried to.

On the great issues of destiny confronting the world's human population today, that swirling and fractious disorder may still sometimes harbor within it sounder judgments than the current consensus of the boards of giant multinational extractive industries and energy suppliers, or even the harassed custodians of public budgets, do. That too is part of democracy's disorientation and makes it ever more urgent to identify better how to distinguish its widening sensitization of our collective judgment to what we need to learn to recognize and take account of from its evident propensity to weaken and bemuse authority. The resulting befuddlement and loss of nerve imperils the capacity of those who precariously hold authority to reach stable judgments on many of the most drastic challenges that face us, or to convince their fellow citizens of the cogency of the judgments they have reached where they do contrive to. The issue of how to judge well together remains as fundamental as ever in human collective life, and we have made remarkably little progress in recognizing why we continue to do it so erratically or why the judgments that govern our most consequential collective actions, on the largest scale on which we can yet decide to act, still often have such calamitous consequences. Why do the people of the United States still squander such a bewildering proportion of their incomes on spectacularly inefficient provision for the health of most of their number, or find it so impossible to discipline their energy consumption to promise their children or grandchildren a less evidently dangerous and profligate future? All of these questions, of course, have well-formed answers, tailored to fit a variety of tastes, some of them worked out with great professional care and ingenuity in recent years. What matters in this context is what it is about democracy as an idea, which means that however carefully and cogently those answers are worked out, no one can rationally be confident that their discovery will transform outcomes in the political world.

All this too is part of democracy's disorientation—the degree to which it confuses our efforts to judge collectively and the intimidating impact of the consequences of that confusion on our disposition even to try to. Where a human population knows just where it is from its own point of view and can see just what it has to choose, there is nothing about democracy that ensures it must disorientate that population or impair its capacity to make up its mind and act accordingly. Arguably, in many ways and for quite a long time, the demos of Athens found themselves in that happy position;[6] and it is certainly possible to tell the political history of the United States, Britain, France, or even the Federal Republic of Germany, over chosen periods, so that their populations too come out as steadily orientated through those institutions and correspondingly equipped to decide democratically to act as they have good reason to. But to tell the story of any community in those terms, you have to pick your dates with some care: not start too early or carry on too long; and even then, it is never right to attribute the felicity of their orientation to the mode in which they took their decisions. That felicity has to be there in the structure of their collective lives, and in the antecedent clarity and, in some sense, also in the validity of their current judgments. As a mechanism of decision, democracy itself can never provide that orientation. At best, it registers and enacts an orientation that is already there. Where there is no such reasonably convergent orientation (no clear common interest), what emerges from democratic decision is either contingent confusion or, at best, a lucky fluke. This may seem a very old-fashioned way of thinking and conspicuously politically incorrect. But newer fashions have been ill-advised to shrug it aside. It certainly does not mean that any aspiring autocrat will prove a good bet, still less that autocracy as such is a bet with any merit at all. It merely means that the world of politics remains a very dangerous place and that we have been exceedingly foolish to see democracy's recent advances as an effective way to remove or diminish those dangers.

There is something powerful and inspiring about democracy's passage through modern world history, something about the ideas that the term, in its transmission between languages, has conjured up, which has strengthened myriads of grievously oppressed human beings in the face of the pain and suffering meted out to them by those who rule or exploit them. That strengthening has made it a source, as well as a vector, of power. But the reinforcement that power has given to democracy as a mode of political legitimation and a set of institutional forms has conspicuously failed to render it a particularly helpful guide to what any human population is well advised to do. This curt judgment profanes one of the principal pieties of many of today's societies but scarcely clashes with the bulk of political experience over time in any society at all. There is little reason to anticipate that it will come to do so anywhere in the future. Why should such a commonplace observation have come to seem so profane?

Part of what has made it sound so is a shift in the meaning of the term over the last century and a half. No speaker of classical Greek of whom we are aware understood the term *demokratia* as a synonym for good government, though many Greeks certainly favored democracy in their sense as the form of government for their own polis (and often for other poleis too). But in the political speech of increasingly many countries across the world today, the United States most consequentially of all, democracy has come often to be heard and meant precisely as good government, not in the sense of government with reliably desirable consequences, but in the sense of government exercised on a wholly appropriate basis and through unimpeachable means, government fully sanctioned by the people and exerted in the spirit and through modes that the latter have explicitly chosen or through means they would definitely welcome. So heard, democracy is unmistakably a critical category and one usually at some distance from the existing dispersion of opinion among the population at large. But *democracy* is also—and in the speech of just the same people—the conventional term for the political order through which they find themselves ruled and which all too frequently conflicts agonizingly with many of their most urgent purposes and deepest commitments.

A term that equivocates in this way, between an authoritative standard of right conduct and the practical character of an existing regime, is a ready source of confusion even for those professionally dedicated to keeping their own thinking and speech clear. In active use, in the rough and tumble of political life, it is all but certain to confuse a great many. Is American government today so confused, so fractious, and so dysfunctional despite democracy or because of democracy? You can make the case either way, depending on how you happen to hear the term. What you cannot readily hope to do is remove either the confusion, the fractiousness, or the dysfunctionality by establishing the superior credentials of your own terminological choice. So the political question of who or what exactly is responsible for the confusion, fractiousness, or dysfunctionality is left untouched by the terminological quarrel; while the fractiousness itself is further exacerbated by the sense that political opponents must be either confused or dishonest, as well as already adhesively in the wrong.

It is not hard to see how the confusion has arisen. The core presumption and central political appeal of the form of government we now habitually call democracy is to embody, or at least seek to realize, a way of reaching political decisions that is fair to every citizen because it treats each equally. The symbolic form of that commitment today is the notionally equal vote, equal not merely in entitlement but also in its prospective causal efficacy. That is certainly a better symbol than no vote at all, or votes that are explicitly weighted unequally on one ground or another. But that notionally equal vote enters, fleetingly and at very lengthy intervals, a dense domain of very active causality, little of which is discernibly structured through any mode of equality at all and which consequently is seldom reshaped in any evident way by that entry and almost never in ways that plainly matter or have much lasting effect.

This could scarcely be otherwise in an ever more capitalist world, where only linguistic habit still sustains the illusion that any of us can see how it could be reconstructed on a quite different footing. Expressed abstractly enough, equal votes remain a more plausible proxy for a fairer basis on which a human grouping makes the decisions it must than any rival basis of comparable existential immediacy or imaginative intelligibility. But any modern state at all, let alone a state on the scale of the United States, continuously makes and struggles to enforce a stunning number of decisions, all of them in conditions of great prior determinacy. The decisions its citizens make when they cast their votes disappear into that bedlam of largely frustrated exertion with startling rapidity, often leaving no recognizable trace at the level of outcome. Neither the decisions that are in the end made, nor the basis on which they have in fact been decided, not even the competing frameworks of assessment that furnish their most potent contributors with the grounds and justifications for aiming as they have, carry through with any clarity or directness to those on whose behalf they are being made and who, between them, must presumptively have authorized the decisions to be made in their name. The result certainly feels like being ruled, as it plainly is, if on a somewhat inscrutable basis. What it never feels like, and equally plainly is not, is "ruling by turns."[7]

The presumption of authorization, however, is not just a polite fiction, as it plausibly still is in China and certainly appeared to be in Egypt under the presidency of Hosni Mubarak. It certainly is polite, and it very largely is a fiction, but it is a fiction with weighty consequences. Some of those consequences stem from the respect in which it is not a fiction at all. They arise from the impact of the point of affirming it on the incentives of the politicians who choose to do so; and they give the best grounds for regarding it as an appropriate label for the form of government in question. What is decisive there is the direction of causality. Where the politicians' grounds for acting as they do are the known prior choices of the majority of the demos, and the rewards the politicians anticipate from being seen to implement those choices, democracy is an impeccable name for the basis on which the decisions are made. In these cases there is no practical disparity between the democratic selection of the politicians in question and the democratic choice of the outcome. Over most of the field of representative democracy in action, and especially over that very large proportion of the field that is largely impervious to the interventions of elected politicians, there is no such causal sequence to trace. What happens may happen under democracy's auspices, but it does not happen because of anything democracy intelligibly implies. It just does not arise predictably from the incentive structure of iterative electoral choice.

But if electoral politics in action is so far from hypnotic, if the conditions of political competition and governmental performance under representative democracy are inevitably frustrating, and if the decisions made are usually so faintly expressive of any clear, stable, or firmly assignable purpose, why should it matter whether or not they are made under democracy's auspices? There are plainly circumstances in which it need not matter at all. If the demos happens to be largely of one mind, the politicians they choose or have chosen for them essentially share their tastes, and if the outcomes each favor fail to do net damage, there will be little to defend their choices against, the aegis of democracy will scarcely be in dispute, and few will care whether it is the known prior choices of the demos itself that caused the politicians to choose as they do.

Where it does potentially matter is where the choices at issue are murkier, or where the purposes of the politicians concerned are knowably and sharply at odds with the definite preferences of the majority of the demos. Where no one concerned has much comprehension of what is going on or what is at stake, democracy is as incapacitated as any other political formula to direct choice fairly and for the better. But its presumptive title to act still looms through the murk, encouraging a calm and relaxation that it can do nothing to justify. Where the aegis of democracy definitely does matter greatly is in cases where elected politicians choose resolutely to defy the known prior preferences of most of the demos, defy its presumptive authority by doing so, but still claim its aegis for the choices they proceed to make. Some of those cases can be very clear, and they may have momentous consequences—in Britain's case recently the choice of its then prime minister to join the United States in invading Iraq. Tony Blair has been eager in many contexts to claim the mantle of democracy; but if that decision was compatible with accepting democracy's authority in directing the action of a state, it is hard to see what decision could not be.

If *democracy* has come to be the most potent term of authorization in global political speech, it must be a grave demerit that we have no clear conception of what it authorizes. It is its potency, of course, that makes it so covetable and contentious, but it is certainly not mainly its potency that makes it so hard to police or adjudicate the resulting contentions. What has made it so hard to do that is the equivocation now lodged deeply within the term itself. The maze of contemporary democracy is a prominent feature of the real political world in which very many now live, but it is also an immense tissue of words, and that tissue and the world that enunciates them are now adhesively impacted on one another. They have become a single structure.

A good maze is one in which it is easy to lose your bearings and from which, once you have done so, it can be very hard to get out. In every real maze, there must be at least one way to get out—the route by which you have come in. Plainly we cannot escape the maze of contemporary democracy by retracing our steps. We cannot reverse time, and very few of us wish to return to any ancien régime. We also cannot hope to remove the myriad other sources of confusion in the real political world we inhabit by recognizing the route we have followed to get where we now are. What we could still reasonably hope to do is break the hypnotic spell the term *democracy* now casts by recognizing how it casts that spell. It is by any human standards absurd to have ended up with a single term for judging where we are in the politics of the world, and what to value and strive for within those politics, a term that carries such pretension to authority but also equivocates so uncontrollably between the official regime name for particular states as these actually are and the most appropriate basis for deciding the most important decisions that bear on the life chances of human beings across the globe. Democracy cannot be a good name for the American state and the institutions that structure its public decisions and determine their consequences, and a good name too, for the basis on which it would be just for the world's human population to decide together what the future should hold for them all. You can question whether democracy has proved a good choice for picking out either of those domains, but you cannot reasonably defend the judgment that anything at all could prove a good choice for picking out both at once. No single term or concept could be a good candidate for picking out even the second, though justice and utility have each had very good runs for their money. The demands for justice have always been quite distinct from the appeals of utility. *Fiat justitia et ruat coelum*—"Let justice be done even if the heavens fall"—is not a utilitarian slogan. For us today the fall of the heavens is all too apt a metaphor for the fate we are still insistently, if inadvertently, bringing on ourselves.

If democracy is a form of government, an institutional structure at a minimum, for determining and implementing the direction of legitimate coercion within a given territory and over a given population, it will have no reliable ties to either justice or utility, and there is no obvious *ex ante* reason to expect it to converge on either, more if it succeeds in getting its way than if it fails. If there was a way to determine conclusively what should be done, by anyone or everyone, to allocate human life chances across the world, that way would carry authority against any possible form of government as well as against every actual government already loose in the world. But there is no such way, and in its absence, what we most need political categories for is to police and direct the governments we do have to decide and act less harmfully than they have yet learned how to.

In that endless and necessarily frustrating struggle—our democratic maze—it has become extremely urgent to recognize where democracy as a political idea can still help us to judge better and where it can only deepen our confusion. If we look back along the route that has led us here, democracy can still sharpen our judgment when we apply it to the structure and authorization of particular regimes. It cannot help us to judge anything if we insist on conceiving it as a legitimatory basis for individual decisions on any but the smallest scale. What to do and avoid doing in the world depends ineliminably on the consequences of acting in one way rather than another. The merits of any way of taking any particular decision cannot be impervious to its consequences in use. It is certainly a merit of a decision that it is made on an appropriate basis and by appropriate means, and the idea of democracy can cast a little light on what bases and means might be appropriate. At least it can pick out some bases for taking decisions and some means for reaching them that are quite clearly inappropriate. (In the case of the British decision to invade Iraq alongside the United States, the moral conviction of the individual political agent who made it, however popular at earlier points in his political career, was always a very poor candidate for vindicating the merits of any decision at all.) On whatever basis a decision is made, even if it carries the active consent of the great majority of a population, it must be a weightier and more decisive merit for it to prove beneficial in the world.

In itself that is scarcely contentious. What is more at issue is why it matters so much for the political bearing of democracy's uneasy presence in the world today. What makes it so important now is principally the intense confusion of our way of thinking about the politics of the world in which we live and the alarmingly ill-conceived character of so much that we obstinately continue to do. It would be encouraging to believe that the second of those grounds, our dismaying collective fecklessness on the scale of individual states, massively compounded by the interactions between states in an overwhelmingly opaque global economy, is principally a consequence of the confusion in the way we think. But that, alas, is not so. It might even be true that there is no connection between the confusion of our thought processes and the infelicity of our cumulative interactions; but there is every reason to doubt that that can be true, either, and it is certainly more within our reach to diminish the confusion of our own thought processes than to bring the unintended consequences of our actions under firmer intentional control, let alone do so with the consequences, evidently unintended by anyone at all, of our cumulative interactions with one another on the scale of the entire globe. With the havoc carried by the vicissitudes of democracy, we can hope to do better.

Many aspects of the predicament in which we find ourselves are highly intractable. Collective action very much remains, and is certain to continue to prove, an inherently puzzling project. There is good reason for game theory to loom so large in the training of political scientists. Much of our current predicament still comes less from being unable to see what to do than from being reluctant to do it. But over and above the dilemmas of collective action and our deep-seated preferences for short-term comfort and convenience over long-term security and flourishing, one other key element that principally reconciles us to that unhappy morass is its pseudo-democratic provenance. The reluctance to make our lives less comfortable and convenient, pandered to with indefatigable ingenuity and assiduity throughout the organization of our economic life, is not a feature of human preference that we can readily modify. What might alter our current weightings is a somewhat better apprehension of the magnitude of the risks we are choosing to run and the brevity of the time scale over which we have thus far chosen to run them.

To judge these better before it is too late is a challenge scientific inquiry may or may not prove able to meet. But even if that essentially cognitive challenge can be met, we have already shown ourselves very poorly organized to convert that gain in comprehension into effective political action.[8] The maze of democracy today is not merely an intellectual embarrassment. It is also already a clear and present political threat, and in prospect it is increasingly likely to prove a biological disaster.

One product of the professionalized and commoditized politics in the democracies of today and the division of political labor in which these result is the pseudo-democratic authorization in that world of the huge bulk of overt public decisions that even purport to carry democratic authorization, and the unremittingly pseudo-democratic authorization of the entire structure of covert or inadvertent decision and nondecision within which those overt decisions nest.

In this setting, the predication of democracy has become overwhelming sedative and disinformative. To block its narcotic impact and restore some clarity, if only at the level of authorization, to what is going on, we would have to relearn our verbal habits and reconstruct our thinking quite fiercely. Under careful scrutiny, that pseudo-democratic provenance rests on nothing more than a feeble pun. There are criteria for decisions being democratic, but those criteria quite evidently do not apply even to the vast majority of overt public decisions in the United States of America, and it is hard to see how they could be thought to apply to covert decisions or inadvertent decisions anywhere at all. To block the anesthetic effect of pseudo-democratic authorization of almost everything the United States or any of its contemporary counterparts does as a state, we need to recognize that democracy cannot plausibly be predicated of particular decisions at all except under conditions so restrictive that they can scarcely be inserted into the ongoing life of a state. If we did choose to deploy the democratic predicate more parsimoniously and precisely to discriminate between regimes as a whole, and ceased to overstretch it fatally to apply to particular state actions, we could position ourselves to think more clearly about the challenges that confront us and the resources we have to meet them. We could also hope to retain on a coherent basis the conviction that the states of which we are citizens are authorized, and possess governments that have been authorized, in a way and a sense in which the states of China's citizens or the subjects of the Kingdom of Saudi Arabia still are not. Even that conviction must be heavily qualified.

Democratic states, like every other form of state, view themselves as authorized well beyond any identifiable warrant. As Hobbes helpfully explained several centuries ago, that claim is one a state must make if it is to furnish the services that give it its raison d'être.[9]

It has to be free and empowered to decide, and it has to be entitled, within some internal system of self-understanding, to enforce what it does decide. But that is a political principle, not an epistemic inference. It says nothing about the prospective merits of the decisions in question. In Hobbes's own way of looking at the matter, just the same must be true of the decisions of what we would think of as a democratic state, even if Hobbes himself might have viewed the latter with special suspicion. What carries the authority is the entitlement and responsibility to decide, not the content of the decisions reached. Subsequent thinking, including some influential recent lines of thought, have fudged to a hazardous degree the relation between entitlement and content.

You can see why this matters if you consider the question of whether there is greater reason for confidence in the public decisions of the United States or India than there is in those of the People's Republic of China. The latter's decisions under the agency that currently rules it have often proved extremely ill-advised, and no one could plausibly claim them to have been, in our sense, authorized by the people they dominate. They do not emanate from a context of free public discussion, and they are made and implemented under circumstances that are sometimes acutely oppressive and where those whom they oppress have no credible hope of a remedy. But does that necessarily make them (and how far has it actually made them) less felicitous in their public impact on the life chances of most of China's population than the corresponding decisions of America's governments over the last three decades have proved for most Americans? If (or insofar as) it has made them less so, what that shows is at most a weak probability relation between the ultimate authorization of political authority and the prospective quality of particular state decisions. No one has yet advanced an argument that establishes that impact as consistently to the advantage of democratic states. That is no reason for favoring autocracy, and it does nothing to render personal oppression less odious. But it is a reason to recognize that nothing about the authority that stands behind the public decisions in contemporary democracies can raise either those decisions or their consequences above suspicion. Since democratic governments see and feel their own authorization with greater confidence and speak about it, if anything, even more effusively than their more autocratic rivals, that judgment matters, and it will matter especially whenever the decisions in question have results that are unmistakably malign.

What the disparities between pretension and justification reflect in this case is the far greater political cogency of democracy as a paradigm for deauthorizing incumbent power than for authorizing it. Democracy deauthorizes incumbency whenever it rejects particular incumbents. As large areas of the world have seen once again as the third millennium opens, it can do so every bit as incisively on the streets as through the ballot box. What it cannot ever do with comparable conclusiveness is authorize particular holders of power, and what it can virtually never do is authorize particular state decisions unless the parameters of these are luminously clear in themselves and can be put in that form to a demos genuinely equipped to understand them. It is especially implausible to see iterative mass suffrage elections, even under conditions of uncoerced participation, and unconstrained and effectively equalized opportunity for the citizens to communicate and inform themselves as yet unmet in any modern state, as authorizing the particular decisions their victors proceed to make.

I have argued that we need to learn to understand democracy very differently: to see it more clearly, hear it with less self-congratulatory ears, recognize more accurately where its real potency comes from, and face up to the limits of its capacity to direct our political purposes. To do so, we need now to take in the historical process that has inserted democracy so prominently into the way we see and feel politics and struggle to understand it. More hazardously and ambitiously, I argue that our cumulative failure to do any of these things gravely aggravates many of the worst dangers that now menace us as a species. We need to find a way out of the maze democracy has become for us and face the awesome decisions that lie ahead as directly and lucidly as we can.

That need is constantly rising in urgency, but it does not rise uniformly or at the same steady pace. In the autumn of 2008, the pace at which it rose accelerated dramatically in the face of three massive and very different kinds of threat. The first was the spreading havoc unleashed by the turmoil in global financial markets, a product of startling levels of indiscretion and cumulatively disinhibited greed.[10] The second, also obtrusively human in origin, has stretched out by now across the Maghreb from Morocco to Egypt and extends north through Syria and east along the Persian Gulf. The third, at its inception, was as brutally extra-human as natural processes come, and concentrated in its impact on the northern island of Japan. All three events will have huge and lasting political consequences, the shape of which we can as yet barely guess. Each shows something fundamental about the constituents of the democratic maze. The popular uprisings rippling out across the Arabic-speaking world demonstrated once again and unforgettably the charismatic force of democracy in deauthorizing incumbent rulers and regimes. The bravery and stoicism with which Japan's people responded to the havoc that overwhelmed them was there long before any of their ancestors had heard the term *democracy*, but even that deep cultural and social strength wilted painfully before the profound failure to organize the material foundations of their lives on a safe and accountable basis, which their deeply entrenched local interpretation of democracy showed up under this savagely extra-human pressure. Many have attributed that failure to the weakness of that realization of democracy—its unusually insulated, parochial, self-serving, and dynastic career-politics milieu, and the latter's continuing subordination to a bureaucratic state apparatus that long preceded it and that is still authorized from most citizens' point of view on far more archaic lines. But the milieu merely expresses more blatantly elements central to the career politics of every existing representative democracy; and the deep failure of Japan's state, in its bureaucratic as much as its democratic aspects, was essentially cognitive: its abject failure to recognize and provide for the scale of risks it had chosen to run. Even on the democratic side, that failure was an index more of the cowardice and impotence of the milieu of professional politics than of any improper potency, set against the rest of the population. You do not need to be powerful to remain comfortably corrupt; but you do need power to make and implement costly decisions for which most citizens will always remain acutely reluctant to recognize the necessity. It has been some time since any Japanese government has held power of that kind.

The blood-stained sands of Libya and the rubble of Syrian cities are vivid marks of democracy's power and vulnerability as a category of political orientation. Bringing down a tyrannical regime by breaking its imagined authority once and for all is an elating political experience, but it goes very little distance toward rebuilding a new regime with a fresh imaginative authority of its own.[11] As Mohamed Morsi, speaking as president-elect of Egypt, told tens of thousands of supporters in Tahrir Square on the eve of his inauguration: "The ministers, the government, the army, the police, all are listening to me when I say no power is above this power, no power is above you. You are the rulers. You are the source of this power and authority."[12] Some assuredly listened less attentively than others, but no one in Egypt could any longer afford to ignore what he was pointing out. Watching the violent reimposition of autocratic rule on even part of a people that had escaped it is a rending experience, since by then the resulting struggle can only take the form of a civil war. Civil wars, as Americans know all too well, have no real victors, though they certainly have losers. Seen clearly, democracy cannot provide a license to enter other peoples' civil wars, even on the side of those who claim its mantle, though it offers more excuse for doing so than for starting a civil war that it has no means to bring to an end. What slender license there was to intervene in Libya came not from the claims of democracy but from the duty to try, insofar as any of us can, to protect fellow human beings from being murdered in very large numbers. That duty requires the capacity to provide the protection (which we may always in the end prove not to possess). Where it does apply, it applies as much where those who are being gunned down or hacked to pieces are friends of the avenging autocrats as to their democratic challengers. It cannot rest on prior political preference.

The more haunting symbol of democracy's current disorientation is the ruined cooling towers of Fukushima. In Fukushima, more vividly and concretely than anywhere else on earth before, it becomes clear how urgently we need to reconsider and reengineer the entire causal web within which our species now lives. We can see how extraordinarily difficult it is to understand that web, and how baffling it is bound to prove to work out together what we now need to do, in and to and with it, and to decide as we do so how to assign the costs of doing it. Once we focus on that, we can readily see how epically unsuited to addressing any of these tasks the political regimes we have fashioned under democracy's aegis now are.

The anguish of Syria, and the scanty and clumsy instruments we possess for attempting to allay it, are certainly something to dwell on, but they are not the only thing to dwell on now. Even in one of democracy's darkest hours, it is every bit as urgent to recognize where the political institutions we have inherited are now failing us in the leading societies of the West, and we are failing ourselves and our descendants in failing to grasp just how and why they are doing so, and how much of what is causing them to do so has infiltrated and taken over our habits of thinking, speaking, and feeling about politics. The democratic maze is part of the world, all right. But it is also and primarily the assemblage of those habits. Since we cannot escape the world itself, and since so many of those habits confine and impede us in handling its challenges, we direly need to reach out beyond them to less narcissistic and parochial forms of understanding and train ourselves to do better.

But how to do so? That is a task, above all, for the world's great universities, since it is there, if anywhere, that people now gather in substantial numbers with time to consider these questions carefully, freedom to consider them frankly, and the ability to begin to understand them less abjectly as they really are. Every distinct aspect is already the focus of deep and disciplined inquiry in institutions well focused for the purpose. But it is wrong to view these distinct aspects synoptically just as a static sum. Each is a single, highly unstable process and all act incessantly upon one another. Among them, the contribution of politics is both especially hard to grasp and quite evidently strategically central. As yet, the discipline of political science has had little success in showing how to grasp it and has made no discernible contribution to showing how to respond to it.[13] The scientific epistemic rubric that increasingly dominates the profession in North America virtually precludes its practitioners from viewing it synoptically and can only discourage their more responsive pupils from attempting to view it that way. It can cast ample light in detail on why things are unlikely to get better in a hurry; but on how to cause them to do so, it is virtually sworn to a lofty and self-righteous silence.

"Who is to educate the educators?" is an old political question, on a free translation, one of the oldest political questions of which Western populations are still aware. It is a mistake to suppose that it is any less urgent a question for a democracy, and a mistake about the gravity of our present ecological and political predicament not to recognize how awesomely that predicament raises its urgency now. Whatever else a great university achieves today, and for all its dazzling variety and accumulated prowess, it should send every one of its pupils out into the world understanding at least that. The core of my case is simple. The global ascent of democracy as a vehicle of presumptive legitimacy, once we recognize how and why it has occurred, has so far done as much to aggravate that predicament as it yet has to alleviate it. The perils that issue from that failure have made it a pressing civic responsibility for all of us, and a peremptory professional responsibility for political scientists in particular, to pull the veil of democracy off that predicament and help steady us all to judge what we must now do in the face of the inexorably structured chaos we have made together.

But is that something we could still in fact do? Is our political, and thus our social, economic, and now unmistakably also our biological fate really in our hands? Is the continuing impulse to believe so just an ignominious delusion? One thing to see is that if it is indeed now a delusion, it must have been a delusion throughout the conscious history of our species as a whole. We have acted as we have acted because of what we are like. We have certainly now unleashed many processes that will prove hard if not impossible to bring under human control. But that has been true on a smaller scale throughout our history. It is not a new structural feature of the human condition, just one we have only recently begun to notice with such well-justified alarm. If we can now act effectively in the face of what we have already done, we will have to do so through enhancing our understanding of the nature and cumulative impact of our own actions and of the powers we can create and deploy to halt and reverse innumerable forms of destruction.

I pressed the special role of great universities in addressing this issue now because the lectures I gave in Henry Stimson's memory were given at Yale and *to* Yale as well as *for* Yale; and because Yale is unmistakably a great university, which aspires to educate for the globe and not just for America's elite-in-waiting and those from elsewhere of very high ability whom it can seduce into joining that elite. But is the view that even the greatest of universities can contribute effectively to this common task also just a delusion—a natural and all too narcissistic fantasy of those with the privilege to teach in them and live off them?

Certainly even the greatest of universities cannot win the fiercest of political struggles against interests with the largest stake in carrying on regardless for as long as nature permits. They cannot speak audibly and persuasively as single voices across the common political space of a nation, still less of the whole globe. On all such issues they cannot and should not speak as single voices at all. But their mission is to teach their pupils how to understand and to press the understanding they try to teach as far as they possibly can. (At least the first of those must be the mission of any real university. The second requires very special concentrations of resources to occur at all effectively.) No other current human institution can do that better or could do it quite so well. If our species cannot learn better in them and from them, it is very unlikely to learn at all.

For the present, great universities are privileged sites for human apprehension of the scale and connectedness of the vast challenges we face. They can try to think synoptically and pull together the range of cognitive endeavors needed to do so. All too obviously none of them yet displays a dependable gift for achieving this. But because they are there, and because that is what is needed, and because the need for it is so devastatingly urgent, it must be especially theirs to try to do. Assigning responsibilities never guarantees their discharge. But it is often the best place to start in the face of human emergencies. Could human beings do any better in the face of the chaos they have made together? The answer to that can only be yes. Will they do any better, and, above all, will they do better enough? Quite probably not. But that is not a conclusion that it makes any practical sense to anticipate. A species facing self-extermination, even at a relatively sedate pace, has reasons for altering its behavior. But it will still be the species that chose to act in the ways that created that risk. How far can human beings learn? In the end they will find out.

NOTES

INTRODUCTION

1. Judt, *Postwar.*

2. Fussell, *The Great War and Modern Memory.*

3. The view that it must be possible to distinguish life as it is lived from luck, in some key respects, was the guiding intuition behind the work of Ronald Dworkin (see, for example, *Sovereign Virtue,* which sets it most at odds with John Rawls, *A Theory of Justice*).

4. Cf. Fukuyama, *The End of History and the Last Man;* Fukuyama, *The Origins of Political Order;* Dunn, *The Cunning of Unreason;* Dunn, "Capitalist Democracy"; Dunn, "Democracy and Its Discontents."

5. Dunn, *The Cunning of Unreason.*

ONE DIAGNOSING DEMOCRACY'S POWER

1. Morison, *Turmoil and Tradition.*

2. Dunn, *The Cunning of Unreason;* Dunn, *Setting the People Free.*

3. Dunn, *Setting the People Free,* 71.

4. For the context, see especially Weston, *English Constitutional Theory and the House of Lords, 1556–1832.* Weston prints the relevant sections of *His Majesties Answer to the XIX Propositions of Both Houses of Parliament* (London: Robert Barker, 1642) at pp. 261–65: "The good of Democracy is Liberty, and the Courage and Industry which Liberty begets" (263).

5. M. Hansen, *The Athenian Democracy in the Age of Demosthenes;* M. Hansen, *The Tradition of Ancient Greek Democracy and Its Importance for Modern Democracy;* Raaflaub, *The Discovery of Freedom in Ancient Greece;* Ober, "The Original Meaning of 'Democracy.'"

6. Seel and Smith, *Crown and Parliaments, 1558–1689;* Russell, *The Causes of the English Civil War; The Fall of the British Monarchies; Parliaments and English Politics, 1621–1629;* Sharpe, *The Personal Rule of Charles I;* Kishlansky, "Charles I."

7. Wedgwood, *The Trial of Charles I,* 217.

8. Plato, *The Republic,* 559D–62; Hobbes, *Leviathan.*

9. Dworkin, *Sovereign Virtue.*

10. Tilly, *Democracy* (cf. Dunn, "Democracy," 487).

11. Dunn, "The Politics of Imponderable and Potentially Lethal Judgment for Mortals," esp. 447–50.

12. Ibid., 448–50.

13. Jean-Jacques Rousseau, *Of the Social Contract.* This can never be a literal description of how things are—at most a political proposal for how they might credibly be seen or felt or made. See Bertram, "Rousseau's Legacy in Two Conceptions of the General Will."

14. Dunn, *The Cunning of Unreason,* 3–137.

15. Weber, *Economy and Society,* vol. 1, chap. 3, 212–301, esp. 215–16.

16. Lenin, *"Left-Wing" Communism,* 629.

17. Tocqueville, *Democracy in America.*

18. Dunn, *Setting the People Free,* chap. 1.

19. Hobbes, *De Cive,* X, ix, 136.

20. Sieyès, *Political Writings.* For the context, see Dunn, *Setting the People Free,* 97–111.

21. Sieyès, *Political Writings* ("Essay on Privileges"), esp. 69–90.

22. The Enlightenment was both a political idea and an intellectual and cultural process. Unsurprisingly it has proved exceptionally hard to locate convincingly in time and space. Among influential recent attempts on varying scales are Jonathan Israel's trilogy *Radical Enlightenment, Enlightenment Contested,* and *Democratic Enlightenment,* as well as *A Revolution of the Mind;* Pocock's even-vaster study, *Barbarism and Religion;* of the antecedents and coordinates of Gibbon's *The History of the Decline and Fall of the Roman Empire;* and Robertson's comparison of the Scottish with the Neapolitan experiences (*The Case for the Enlightenment*). Ambitious older construals by Cassirer, *The Philosophy of the Enlightenment,* and Gay, *The Enlightenment,* still have some force. None has contrived to lay to rest Kant's (*Political Writings*) mesmeric question: "What is Enlightenment?"

TWO DEMOCRACY'S ASCENT

1. Most of those, like John Cotton or Richard Mather, who did mention democracy from the 1630s onward, did so in connection with issues of church government, and very few commended its

direct application to the structure of authority, even in that setting. I am very grateful to Teresa Bejan of the Yale Political Science Department for her help in confirming this assessment. For a more external view, largely bracketing the philology, see Maloy, *The Colonial American Origins of Modern Democratic Thought.*

2. Wilentz, *The Rise of American Democracy;* Wood, *The Radicalism of the American Revolution,* but cf. Wood, *The Creation of the American Republic, 1776–1787,* 602–15.

3. Pollock, *The Language of the Gods in the World of Men.*

4. Cook, *Commanding Right and Forbidding Wrong in Islamic Thought.* Also cf. Patricia Crone, *God's Rule;* Black, *The History of Islamic Political Thought;* Watanabe, *A History of Japanese Political Thought, 1600–1901.*

5. Judt, *Postwar,* chap. 1.

6. Keane, *The Life and Death of Democracy.*

7. Ibid.

8. Goody, *The Domestication of the Savage Mind.*

9. Israel, *Radical Enlightenment, Enlightenment Contested,* and *Democratic Enlightenment.*

10. Dunn, *Setting the People Free,* chaps. 3 and 4.

11. Wood, *The Creation of the American Republic.*

12. Hamilton, *The Papers of Alexander Hamilton,* vol. 1, 255. Letter to Gouverneur Morris, 19 May 1777: "A representative democracy, where the right of election is well secured and regulated & the exercise of the legislative, executive and judiciary authorities, is vested in select persons chosen *really* and not *nominally* by the people, will in my opinion be most likely to be happy, regular and durable." This was by no means Hamilton's only tone on the topic of democracy. For his role as hero-villain of the American founding, see, helpfully, Jack Rakove, *Revolutionaries,* chap. 9, and Wood, *Revolutionary Characters,* chap. 4.

13. Rakove, *Revolutionaries,* 170.

14. Cf. Handler, *America and Europe in the Thought of John Adams;* Haraszti, *John Adams and the Prophets of Progress;* Rakove, *Revolutionaries;* Wood, *Revolutionary Characters.*

15. Hoffman et al., *Dear Papa, Dear Charley . . .;* Rakove, *Revolutionaries,* 188.

16. Hamilton, Madison, and Jay, *The Federalist Papers,* 47–53; and see Rakove, *James Madison and the Founding of the American Republic* and *Original Meanings;* Banning, *The Sacred Fire of Liberty;* McEvoy, *The Last of the Fathers.*

17. Rakove, *Revolutionaries,* 386–87.

18. Tocqueville, *Democracy in America.* For the life behind this, see, conveniently, Brogan, *Alexis de Tocqueville.* For a sobering assessment, see Wolin, *Tocqueville Between Two Worlds.*

19. Hartz, *The Liberal Tradition in America;* Hartz et al., *The Founding of New Societies;* cf. Wood, *The Radicalism of the American Revolution* and *The Creation of the American Republic;* Wilentz, *The Rise of American Democracy.*

20. Xiong, "Difficulties in Comprehension and Differences in Expression."

21. Levenson, *Confucian China and Its Modern Fate;* Schwartz, *In Search of Wealth and Power;* Grieder, *Hu Shih and the Chinese Renaissance;* Huang, *The Meaning of Freedom;* and for broader views of the immediate historical setting, see Wang, *Chinese Intellectuals and the West,* 306–421, and Tse-tsung, *The May Fourth Movement.* The most ambitious and pertinacious Western attempt so far to take the measure of the depth of the resulting disagreement has been the work of Metzger. See especially *A Cloud Across the Pacific.*

22. Hsiao, *A History of Chinese Political Thought.* Volume 1 was completed in 1941, but the translation into English did not appear

until 1979, and volume 2 has not yet been finished. Fairbank, *The Chinese World Order;* Chi-Chao, *History of Chinese Political Thought During the Early Tsin Period;* Schwartz, *The World of Thought in Ancient China;* Mote, *Imperial China, 900–1800.* For an instructive comparison with Indian experience, see Ocko and Gilmartin, "State, Sovereignty, and the People."

23. Vogel, *Deng Xiaoping and the Transformation of China.*

24. Vogel, *Deng Xiaoping.* The slogan was criticized by Mao Zedong (Vogel, 164) but conveyed an important element in Deng's approach to governing (Vogel, 391).

25. Cf. Keane, *The Life and Death of Democracy,* 101–26.

26. Hsiao, *A History of Chinese Political Thought.*

27. Burke, *Reflections on the Revolution in France,* 157–58.

28. Rakove, *Original Meanings;* Dunn, "Unmanifest Destiny."

29. Pierson *Tocqueville in America;* Tocqueville, *Journey to America;* Tocqueville, *Letters from America;* Beaumont, *Lettres d'Amérique, 1831–1832.*

30. Vogel, *Deng Xiaoping;* Kirby, *The People's Republic of China at 60;* Helmann and Perry, *Mao's Invisible Hand.*

THREE RECOGNIZING DEMOCRACY'S DISORIENTATION

1. Dikötter, *Mao's Great Famine.*

2. Helmann and Perry, *Mao's Invisible Hand.*

3. Grieder, *Hu Shih and the Chinese Renaissance;* Huang, *The Meaning of Freedom.* For some of the inspiration behind Huang's work, see Metzger, *A Cloud Across the Pacific.*

4. Westbrook, *John Dewey and American Democracy;* Ryan, *John Dewey and the High Tide of American Liberalism.*

5. Hsiao, *A History of Chinese Political Thought.* There were, of course, ample European precedents for views far closer to China's

than America's: Ullmann, *Medieval Political Thought* and *Principles of Government and Politics in the Middle Ages;* Bloch, *The Royal Touch;* Weber, *Economy and Society.*

6. Huntington, *The Clash of Civilizations and the Remaking of World Order.*

7. Bourzhou Daragahi, "Revolutionary Ideals Fade as Egypt Decides," *Financial Times,* June 7, 2012, quoting Wafaa Hassaneen, a forty-seven-year-old woman selling loaves of bread on a Cairo pavement, whose daily income had more than halved since the fall of Mubarak: "The revolution was great for the first eighteen days. But the revolution is no longer. Now it is just clutter."

8. Locke, *Two Treatises of Government,* treatise II, para. 49, p. 319.

9. Xiong, "Difficulties in Comprehension."

10. Ibid., 1–2.

11. Ibid., 3.

12. Ibid.

13. Farrar, "Taking Our Chances with the Ancient Athenians."

14. Levenson, *Confucian China and Its Modern Fate;* Wright, *The Last Stand of Chinese Conservatism;* Kuhn, *Rebellion and Its Enemies in Late Imperial China.*

15. Price, *Russia and the Roots of the Chinese Revolution, 1896–1911;* Meisner, *Li Ta-Chao and the Origins of Chinese Marxism.*

16. Stepan, Linz, and Yadav, *Democracy in Multinational Societies;* Yadav, "Democracy and Poverty in India"; Banerjee, "Sacred Elections."

17. For synoptic accounts, see Visvanathan and Sethi, *Foul Play,* and Brass, *Theft of an Idol.* For closer presentations, see Wade, "The System of Administrative and Political Corruption," and Parry, "The 'Crisis of Corruption' and the 'Idea of India.' "

18. Cf. Bayly, *Recovering Liberties;* Gilmartin, "Towards a Global History of Voting"; Kaviraj, *The Trajectories of the Indian State* and *The Enchantment of Democracy and India.*

19. Guha, *Makers of Modern India.*

20. Parel, *Gandhi's Philosophy and the Quest for Harmony;* Parekh, *Gandhi's Political Philosophy;* Brown, *Gandhi's Rise to Power* and *Gandhi and Civil Disobedience;* cf. Anderson, "Gandhi Centre Stage."

21. Khilnani, *The Idea of India* and "Nehru's Judgment"; Gopal, *Jawaharlal Nehru.*

22. Austin, *The Indian Constitution* and *Working a Democratic Constitution.*

23. Pollock, *The Language of the Gods.* Cf. Ocko and Gilmartin, "State, Sovereignty, and the People."

24. Mill, *On Liberty,* in *Collected Works,* vol. 18, 224.

25. Ibid., 120.

26. Mill, *Considerations on Representative Government,* in *Collected Works,* vol. 19, 395.

27. Ibid., 393–94.

28. Mill, *The History of British India,* vol. 1, 456.

29. Mantena, *Alibis of Empire,* 316; Stephen, *Liberty, Equality, Fraternity,* 68–69.

30. Mantena, *Alibis of Empire.*

31. Kloppenberg, *Uncertain Victory;* Festenstein, *Pragmatism and Political Theory.*

32. Adiga, *The White Tiger;* for an equally stark report, with greater emphasis on the resilience of some of the sufferers, see Boo, *Behind the Beautiful Forevers.*

FOUR RECOVERING OUR BEARINGS

1. Yadav, "Democracy and Poverty in India"; Banerjee, "Sacred Elections."

2. Manor, *Power, Poverty, and Poison;* T. Hansen, *Wages of Violence;* Tarlo, *Unsettling Memories.*

3. Sen, *Poverty and Famines.*

4. Dikötter, *Mao's Great Famine.*

5. Tocqueville, *Democracy in America* and *Journey to America;* Pierson, *Tocqueville in America.*

6. Ober, "The Original Meaning of 'Democracy' "; Finley, *Politics in the Ancient World.*

7. Aristotle, *Politics,* 1317b, 488–89.

8. Dunn, "The Emergence into Politics of Global Environmental Change."

9. Hobbes, *Leviathan.*

10. Lewis, *The Big Short;* Cassidy, *How Markets Fail.*

11. *Financial Times,* London, June 30, 2012, p. 8.

12. Mohamed Morsi speech, Friday, June 29, 2012. For a translation of the full speech, see the Muslim Brotherhood site: www.ikhwanweb.com/article.php?id=30153.

13. Dunn, "The Emergence into Politics."

BIBLIOGRAPHY

Adiga, Aravind. *The White Tiger.* London: Atlantic Books, 2008.

Anderson, Perry. "Gandhi Centre Stage." *London Review of Books* 34, no. 13 (July 5, 2012): 3–11.

Aristotle. *Politics.* Translated by H. Rackham. Cambridge: Harvard University Press, 1932.

Austin, Granville. *The Indian Constitution: Cornerstone of a Nation.* Oxford: Oxford University Press, 1999.

———. *Working a Democratic Constitution: The Indian Experience.* Oxford: Oxford University Press, 1999.

Banerjee, Mukulika. "Sacred Elections." *Economic and Political Weekly* (India) 42, no. 17 (April 28, 2007): 1556–62.

Banning, Lance. *The Sacred Fire of Liberty.* Ithaca: Cornell University Press, 1995.

Bayly, C. A. *Recovering Liberties: Indian Thought in the Age of Liberalism and Empire.* Cambridge: Cambridge University Press, 2012.

Beaumont, Gustave de. *Lettres d'Amérique, 1831–1832.* Paris: Presses Universitaires de France, 1973.

Bertram, Christopher. "Rousseau's Legacy in Two Conceptions of the General Will: Democratic and Transcendent." *Review of Politics* 74, no. 3 (2012): 403–19.

Black, Anthony. *The History of Islamic Political Thought: From the Prophet to the Present.* London: Routledge, 2001.

Bloch, Marc. *The Royal Touch: Sacred Monarchy and Scrofula in England and France.* Translated by J. E. Anderson. London: Routledge & Kegan Paul, 1973.

Boo, Katherine. *Behind the Beautiful Forevers.* London: Portobello Books, 2012.

Bourke, Richard, and Raymond Geuss, eds. *Political Judgment.* Cambridge: Cambridge University Press, 2010.

Brass, Paul. *Theft of an Idol: Text and Context in the Representation of Collective Violence.* Princeton: Princeton University Press, 1997.

Brogan, Hugh. *Alexis de Tocqueville: A Life.* New Haven: Yale University Press, 2007.

Brown, Judith M. *Gandhi and Civil Disobedience: The Mahatma in Indian Politics, 1929–1934.* Cambridge: Cambridge University Press, 1977.

———. *Gandhi's Rise to Power: Indian Politics, 1915–1922.* Cambridge: Cambridge University Press, 1972.

Burke, Edmund. *Reflections on the Revolution in France* (1790). Edited by Frank N. Turner. New Haven: Yale University Press, 2003.

Cassidy, John. *How Markets Fail: The Logic of Economic Calamities.* New York: Farrar, Straus and Giroux, 2009.

Cassirer, Ernst. *The Philosophy of the Enlightenment.* Translated by Fritz C. A. Koelln and James P. Pettegrove. Boston: Beacon Press, 1955.

Chi-Chao, Liang. *History of Chinese Political Thought During the Early Tsin Period.* London: Kegan Paul, 1930.

Cook, Michael A. *Commanding Right and Forbidding Wrong in Islamic Thought.* Cambridge: Cambridge University Press, 2000.

Crone, Patricia. *God's Rule: Government and Islam.* Edinburgh: Edinburgh University Press, 2004.

Dikötter, Frank. *Mao's Great Famine: The History of China's Most Devastating Catastrophe, 1958–1962.* London: Penguin, 2011.

Dunn, John. "Capitalist Democracy: Elective Affinity or Beguiling Illusion?" *Daedalus* 136, no. 3 (2007): 5–13.

———. *The Cunning of Unreason.* London: HarperCollins, 2000.

———. "Democracy and Its Discontents." *National Interest* 106 (March–April 2010): 54–63.

———. "Democracy." *European Journal of Sociology* 49, no. 3 (2008): 487–91.

———. "The Emergence into Politics of Global Environmental Change." In *Encyclopaedia of Global*

Environmental Change, edited by Ted Munn, 124–36. Vol. 5. London: John Wiley, 2002.

———. "The Politics of Imponderable and Potentially Lethal Judgment for Mortals: Hobbes's Legacy to the Understanding of Modern Politics." In *Leviathan,* by Thomas Hobbes, edited by Ian Shapiro, 433–52. New Haven: Yale University Press, 2010.

———. *Setting the People Free: The Story of Democracy.* London: Atlantic Books, 2005.

———. "Unmanifest Destiny." In *The Federalist Papers,* by Alexander Hamilton, James Madison, and John Jay, edited by Ian Shapiro, 483–501. New Haven: Yale University Press, 2009.

Dworkin, Ronald. *Sovereign Virtue: The Theory and Practice of Equality.* Cambridge: Harvard University Press, 2000.

Fairbank, John J. *The Chinese World Order: Traditional China's Foreign Relations.* Cambridge: Harvard University Press, 1968.

Farrar, Cynthia. "Taking Our Chances with the Ancient Athenians." In *Démocratie Athénienne—Démocratie Moderne: Tradition et Influences,* edited by M. H. Hansen, 167–234. Geneva: Hardt Foundation, 2010.

Festenstein, Matthew. *Pragmatism and Political Theory.* Cambridge, U.K.: Polity Press, 1997.

Financial Times, London, June 7 and 30, 2012.

Finley, Moses I. *Politics in the Ancient World.* Cambridge: Cambridge University Press, 1983.

Fukuyama, Francis. *The End of History and the Last Man.* London: Hamish Hamilton, 1992.

———. *The Origins of Political Order: From Prehuman Times to the French Revolution.* London: Profile, 2011.

Fussell, Paul. *The Great War and Modern Memory.* Oxford: Oxford University Press 1975.

Gay, Peter. *The Enlightenment: An Interpretation.* 2 vols. London: Weidenfeld & Nicolson, 1967–1970.

Gibbon, Edward. *The History of the Decline and Fall of the Roman Empire.* Edited by David Womersley. London: Penguin, 2005.

Gilmartin, David. "Towards a Global History of Voting: Sovereignty, the Diffusion of Ideas, and the Enchanted Individual." *Religions* 3 (2012): 407–33.

Goody, Jack. *The Domestication of the Savage Mind.* Cambridge: Cambridge University Press, 1977.

Gopal, Sarvepalli. *Jawaharlal Nehru: A Biography.* 3 vols. Cambridge: Harvard University Press, 1976–1984.

Grieder, Jerome B. *Hu Shih and the Chinese Renaissance: Liberalism in the Chinese Revolution, 1917–1937.* Cambridge: Harvard University Press, 1970.

Guha, Ramachandra. *India After Gandhi: The History of the World's Largest Democracy.* London: Penguin, 2008.

———. *Makers of Modern India.* Cambridge: Harvard University Press, 2009.

Hamilton, Alexander. *The Papers of Alexander Hamilton.* Edited by Harold C. Syrett and Jacob E. Cooke. New York: Columbia University Press, 1961.

Hamilton, Alexander, James Madison, and John Jay. *The Federalist Papers.* Edited by Ian Shapiro. New Haven: Yale University Press, 2009.

Handler, Edward. *America and Europe in the Thought of John Adams.* Cambridge: Harvard University Press, 1964.

Hansen, Mogens H. *The Athenian Democracy in the Age of Demosthenes.* Oxford: Blackwell, 1991.

———. *The Tradition of Ancient Greek Democracy and Its Importance for Modern Democracy.* Copenhagen: Royal Danish Academy of Science and Letters, 2005.

Hansen, Thomas B. *Wages of Violence: Naming and Identity in Postcolonial Bombay.* Princeton: Princeton University Press, 2001.

Haraszti, Zoltan. *John Adams and the Prophets of Progress.* New York: Grosset & Dunlap, 1964.

Hartz, Louis. *The Liberal Tradition in America.* New York: Harcourt, Brace, 1955.

Hartz, Louis, et al. *The Founding of New Societies.* New York: Harcourt, Brace & World, 1964.

Helmann, Sebastian, and Elizabeth J. Perry, eds. *Mao's Invisible Hand: The Political Foundations of Adaptive Government in China.* Cambridge: Harvard University Asia Center, 2012.

Hobbes, Thomas. *De Cive: The English Version.* Edited by Howard Warrender. Oxford: Clarendon Press, 1983.

———. *Leviathan.* 3 vols. Edited by Noel Malcolm. Oxford: Clarendon Press, 2012.

Hoffman, Ronald, et al., eds. *Dear Papa, Dear Charley. . . .* Chapel Hill: University of North Carolina Press, 2001.

Hsiao, Kung-chuan. *A History of Chinese Political Thought.* Vol. 1, *From the Beginnings to the Sixth Century A.D.*, translated by F. W. Mote. Princeton: Princeton University Press, 1979.

Huang, Max Ko-wu. *The Meaning of Freedom: Yan Fu and the Origins of Chinese Liberalism.* Hong Kong: Chinese University Press, 2008.

Huntington, Samuel P. *The Clash of Civilizations and the Remaking of World Order.* New York: Simon & Schuster, 1996.

Israel, Jonathan. *Democratic Enlightenment: Philosophy, Revolution, and Human Rights, 1750–1790.* Oxford: Oxford University Press, 2011.

———. *Enlightenment Contested: Philosophy, Modernity, and the Emancipation of Man, 1670–1752.* Oxford: Oxford University Press, 2006.

———. *Radical Enlightenment: Philosophy and the Making of Modernity, 1650–1750.* Oxford: Oxford University Press, 2001.

———. *A Revolution of the Mind: A Radical Enlightenment and the Intellectual Origins of Modern Democracy.* Oxford: Oxford University Press, 2009.

Judt, Tony. *Postwar.* London: Vintage, 2010.

Kant, Immanuel. *Kant: Political Writings.* Edited by Hans Reiss, translated by H. B. Nisbet. Cambridge: Cambridge University Press, 1970.

Kaviraj, Sudipta. *The Enchantment of Democracy and India.* Ranikhet, India: Permanent Black, 2011.

———. *The Trajectories of the Indian State.* Ranikhet, India: Permanent Black, 2010.

Keane, John. *The Life and Death of Democracy.* New York: W. W. Norton, 2009.

Khilnani, Sunil. *The Idea of India.* London: Hamish Hamilton, 1997.

———. "Nehru's Judgment." In *Political Judgment,* edited by Richard Bourke and Raymond Geuss, 254–77. Cambridge: Cambridge University Press.

Kirby, William C., ed. *The People's Republic of China at 60: An International Assessment.* Cambridge: Harvard University Asia Center, 2011.

Kishlansky, Mark. "Charles I: A Case of Mistaken Identity." *Past & Present* 189, no. 1 (November 2005): 41–80.

Kloppenberg, James T. *Uncertain Victory: Social Democracy and Progressivism in European and American Thought, 1870–1920.* Oxford: Oxford University Press, 1988.

Kuhn, Philip. *Rebellion and Its Enemies in Late Imperial China: Militarization and Social Structure, 1796–1864.* Cambridge: Harvard University Press, 1970.

Lenin, Vladimir I. *"Left-Wing" Communism: An Infantile Disorder.* In *Selected Works,* 2 vols. Moscow: Foreign Languages Publishing House, 1947.

Levenson, Joseph R. *Confucian China and Its Modern Fate.* 3 vols. London: Routledge & Kegan Paul, 1958–1965.

Lewis, Michael. *The Big Short: Inside the Doomsday Machine.* London: Penguin, 2011.

Locke, John. *Two Treatises of Government.* Edited by Peter Laslett. Cambridge: Cambridge University Press, 1960.

Maloy, Jason S. *The Colonial American Origins of Modern Democratic Thought.* Cambridge: Cambridge University Press, 2008.

Manor, James. *Power, Poverty, and Poison: Disaster and Response in an Indian City.* Delhi: Sage Publications, 1993.

Mantena, Karuna. *Alibis of Empire.* Princeton: Princeton University Press, 2009.

McEvoy, Drew R. *The Last of the Fathers: James Madison and the Republican Legacy.* Cambridge: Cambridge University Press, 1989.

Meisner, Maurice J. *Li Ta-Chao and the Origins of Chinese Marxism.* Cambridge: Harvard University Press, 1967.

Metzger, Thomas A. *A Cloud Across the Pacific.* Hong Kong: Chinese University Press, 2005.

Mill, James. *The History of British India.* 6 vols. Indianapolis: Liberty Fund, 1990.

Mill, John Stuart. *Collected Works of John Stuart Mill.* Edited by J. M. Robson. Toronto: University of Toronto Press, 1963–1997.

Mookerji, Radhakamal. *Democracies of the East: A Study in Comparative Politics.* London: P. S. King, 1923.

Morison, Elting E. *Turmoil and Tradition: A Study of the Life and Times of Henry L. Stimson.* Boston: Houghton Mifflin, 1960.

Mote, F. W. *Imperial China, 900–1800.* Cambridge: Harvard University Press, 2003.

Ober, Josiah. "The Original Meaning of 'Democracy': Capacity to Do Things, Not Majority Rule." *Constellations* 15, no. 1 (2008): 3–9.

Ocko, Jonathan K., and David Gilmartin. "State, Sovereignty, and the People: A Comparison of the 'Rule of Law' in China and India." *Journal of Asian Studies* 68 no. 1 (2009): 55–100.

Parekh, Bhikhu C. *Gandhi's Political Philosophy: A Critical Examination.* Notre Dame: University of Notre Dame Press, 1989.

Parel, Anthony. *Gandhi's Philosophy and the Quest for Harmony.* Cambridge: Cambridge University Press, 2006.

Parry, Jonathan. "The 'Crisis of Corruption' and the 'Idea of India': A Worm's Eye View." In *The Morals of Legitimacy: Between Agency and System,* edited by Italo Pardo, 27–56. Oxford, U.K.: Berghahn Books, 2000.

Pierson, George Wilson. *Tocqueville in America.* Baltimore: Johns Hopkins University Press, 1996 [1938].

Plato. *The Republic.* Translated by Paul Shorey. Cambridge: Harvard University Press, 1930–1935.

Pocock, J. G. A. *Barbarism and Religion.* 5 vols. to date. Cambridge: Cambridge University Press, 1999–2011.

Pollock, Sheldon. *The Language of the Gods in the World of Men: Sanskrit, Culture, and Power in Premodern India.* Berkeley: University of California Press, 2006.

Price, Don C. *Russia and the Roots of the Chinese Revolution, 1896–1911.* Cambridge: Harvard University Press, 1974.

Raaflaub, Kurt. *The Discovery of Freedom in Ancient Greece.* Revised and updated ed. Chicago: University of Chicago Press, 2004.

Rakove, Jack. *James Madison and the Founding of the American Republic.* 2nd ed. New York: Longman, 2002.

———. *Original Meanings: Politics and Ideas in the Making of the Constitution.* New York: Vintage, 1997.

———. *Revolutionaries: Inventing an American Nation.* London: William Heinemann, 2010.

Rawls, John. *A Theory of Justice.* Cambridge: Harvard University Press, 1971.

Robertson, John. *The Case for the Enlightenment: Scotland and Naples, 1680–1760.* Cambridge: Cambridge University Press, 2005.

Rousseau, Jean-Jacques. *Of the Social Contract.* In *The Social Contract and Other Later Political Writings,* edited by Victor Gourevitch. Cambridge: Cambridge University Press, 1997.

Russell, Conrad. *The Causes of the English Civil War: The Ford Lectures Delivered in the University of Oxford.* Oxford: Clarendon Press, 1990.

———. *The Fall of the British Monarchies.* Oxford: Clarendon Press, 1991.

———. *Parliaments and English Politics, 1621–1629.* Oxford: Clarendon Press, 1982.

Ryan, Alan. *John Dewey and the High Tide of American Liberalism.* New York: W. W. Norton, 1995.

Schwartz, Benjamin I. *In Search of Wealth and Power.* New York: Harper, 1964.

———. *The World of Thought in Ancient China.* Cambridge: Belknap Press, 1985.

Seel, Graham E., and David L. Smith. *Crown and Parliaments, 1558–1689.* Cambridge: Cambridge University Press, 2001.

Sen, Amartya. *Poverty and Famines: An Essay on Entitlement and Deprivation.* Oxford: Clarendon Press, 1981.

Sharpe, Kevin. *The Personal Rule of Charles I.* New Haven: Yale University Press, 1992.

Sieyès, Emmanuel J. *Political Writings.* Edited by Michael Sonenscher. Indianapolis: Hackett, 2003.

Stepan, Alfred, Juan J. Linz, and Yogendra Yadav. *Democracy in Multinational Societies: India and Other Polities.* Baltimore: Johns Hopkins University Press, 2010.

Stephen, James Fitzjames. *Liberty, Equality, Fraternity.* Indianapolis: Liberty Fund, 1993.

Tarlo, Emma. *Unsettling Memories: Narratives of the Emergency in Delhi.* London: Hurst, 2003.

Tilly, Charles. *Democracy.* Cambridge: Cambridge University Press, 2007.

Tocqueville, Alexis de. *Democracy in America.* Translated by Harvey C. Mansfield and Delba Winthrop. Chicago: University of Chicago Press, 2000.

———. *Journey to America.* Edited by J. P. Mayer. London: Faber & Faber, 1959.

———. *Letters from America.* Edited and translated by Frederick Brown. New Haven: Yale University Press, 2010.

Tse-tsung, Chow. *The May Fourth Movement: Intellectual Revolution in Modern China.* Cambridge: Harvard University Press, 1960.

Ullmann, Walter. *Medieval Political Thought.* London: Penguin, 1975.

———. *Principles of Government and Politics in the Middle Ages.* London: Methuen, 1966.

Visvanathan, Shiv, and Harsh Sethi, eds. *Foul Play: Chronicles of Corruption, 1947–1997.* New Delhi: Banyan Books, 1998.

Vogel, Ezra F. *Deng Xiaoping and the Transformation of China.* Cambridge: Harvard University Press, 2011.

Wade, Robert. "The System of Administrative and Political Corruption: Canal Irrigation in South India." *Journal of Development Studies* 18 (1982): 287–328.

Wang, Y. C. *Chinese Intellectuals and the West.* Chapel Hill: University of North Carolina Press, 1966.

Watanabe, Hiroshi. *A History of Japanese Political Thought, 1600–1901.* Translated by David Noble. Tokyo: I-House Press, 2012.

Weber, Max. *Economy and Society: An Outline of Interpretive Sociology.* Edited by Guenther Roth and Claus Wittich. 3 vols. New York: Bedminster Press, 1968.

Wedgwood, C. Veronica. *The Trial of Charles I.* London: Fontana, 1964.

Westbrook, Robert B. *John Dewey and American Democracy.* Ithaca: Cornell University Press, 1991.

Weston, Corinne C. *English Constitutional Theory and the House of Lords, 1556–1832.* London: Routledge & Kegan Paul, 1965.

Wilentz, Sean. *The Rise of American Democracy: Jefferson to Lincoln.* New York: W. W. Norton, 2007.

Wolin, Sheldon S. *Tocqueville Between Two Worlds.* Princeton: Princeton University Press, 2001.

Wood, Gordon S. *The Creation of the American Republic, 1776–1787.* New York: W. W. Norton, 1972.

———. *The Radicalism of the American Revolution.* New York: Vintage, 1993.

———. *Revolutionary Characters: What Made the Founders Different.* London: Penguin, 2007.

Wright, Mary. *The Last Stand of Chinese Conservatism: The T'ung-Chi Restoration, 1862–1874.* New York: Atheneum, 1966.

Xiong, Yuezhi. "Difficulties in Comprehension and Differences in Expression: Interpreting American Democracy in the Late Qing." *Late Imperial China* 23, no. 1 (2002): 1–27.

Yadav, Yogendra. "Democracy and Poverty in India." In *Indian Democracy: Problems and Prospects,* edited by Sharmila Mitra Deb and M. Manisha. New Delhi: Anthem Press, 2009.

INDEX